Model-Based Business Engineering
Successful Model Development and Use

Model-Based-Business-Engineering
Dr. Juergen Pitschke

Successful Model Development and Use
Notations, Methods, Techniques

2. Edition, English

Dr. Juergen Pitschke
BCS – Dr. Juergen Pitschke
buch@enterprise-design.eu

All trademarks and product names mentioned in this book are subject to trademark, trademark, or patent protection or are trademarks or registered trademarks of their respective owners. The reproduction of trademarks, product names, trade names, trade names, trade names, etc. in this work, even without labeling, does not justify the assumption that such names should be considered free for the purposes of trademark or trademark protection and should therefore be used by anyone.

This publication is protected by copyright. All rights reserved.

All information in this book has been checked with the utmost care. However, neither the author nor publisher can be held liable for any damages incurred in connection with the use of this book.

Copyright © 2020 Dr. Juergen Pitschke

Foreword

Last year I published my second book ((J. Pitschke, Model-Based Business Engineering: Successful Model Development and Use 2019)). The idea was to use the possibilities of self-publishing (ongoing updates). As a result, new content has been added continuously. However, the golden thread has been lost.

Therefore, I plan to extend the book in the style of blog posts about notations, methods, architecture. The existing content of the book is the base (Part I). It will be extended by further content and ideas. Many posts you can also find in my blog (www.model-based-business.engineering).

I hope you enjoy and find inspiration for your work. I look forward to your feedback and requests for additions.

Thanks also to my son Clemens and Kathrin Schild for their support.

Juergen Pitschke
Dresden, May 2020

Content

1 Model-Based Business Engineering 10
    1.1 Model-Based 10
    1.2 Why models? 11
    1.2.1 What is a Model? 11
    1.2.2 Presenting Models - Formal (Standard-)Notations 11
    1.2.3 Presenting Models - Informal Descriptions 12
    1.2.4 Language 12
    1.2.5 Model and Model-Output 13
    1.3 Content, Comprehension, and Form of Presentation 14
    1.3.1 What should be in a model? Primary and secondary Model content 14
    1.3.2 Organize Primary Model Content 16
    1.3.3 Secondary Model Content 16
    1.4 ... Business 17
    1.4.1 Business – What is the subject of interest? 17
    1.4.2 Business and IT – What is the role of technology in Model-Based Business Engineering? 18
    1.5 ... Business Engineering – Develop Business Capabilities systematically 19
    1.5.1 Standard-Notations, informal Descriptions, Styleguides 19
    1.5.2 Modeling and Working Techniques 19
    1.6 Business Engineering is People Business 20
    1.6.1 Continues Improvement and Model Governance 20
    1.7 Business Process Models and Structure 20
    1.8 Structure, Structure, Structure 21

2 The Zachman-Framework for Enterprise Architecture™ 23
    2.1 Content in the Zachman-Framework 24
    2.2 Detail Level 26
    2.3 What is the purpose of a Model? 29
    2.4 Notations for Enterprise Modeling 31

3 Process Maps, Process Houses and other overviews 38
    3.1 Motivational Elements 40
    3.2 Business Motivation Model 40

4 Introduction to SBVR – The Vocabulary 44
    4.1 Concepts and Terms, Synonym, Communities 44
    4.2 Facts and Fact Types 45
    4.3 Presentation of a Vocabulary 46
    4.4 Finding Terms and Facts for a Vocabulary 47

5 Describing Business Processes 49
    5.1 What is a Business Process? Types of Business Processes, Presentation forms 49
    5.2 Describing Business Processes – BPMN 50
    5.3 Describing Business Processes – CMMN 52
    5.4 Operative Business Decisions and Business Rules 58
    5.4.1 Operative Business Decisions – DMN und TDM 59
    5.4.2 DMN Palette 61
    5.4.3 DMN-Element Decision 61
    5.4.4 DMN-Elements Input and Sub decisions 62
    5.4.5 DMN-Element Knowledge Model 62

- 5.4.6 DMN-Element Knowledge Source 62
- 5.4.7 Additional information for business decisions 63
- 5.4.8 TDM methodology 64
- 5.4.9 Describing business rules in natural language 64
- 5.5 Describing Business Processes – IGOE Concept, RACI-Charts, other descriptions 64
- 5.5.1 The IGOE concept 65
- 5.5.2 RACI-Charts– Responsibilities in the Business Process 66
- 5.5.3 Business Processes and Risk Assessment 67
- 5.5.4 Customer Journey Maps 68
- 5.5.5 Other descriptions 69
- 5.6 Describing Organization Structures 70
- 5.7 Business Capabilities 70
- 5.8 Describe Business Processes - Business Process Pattern 73
- 5.8.1 Definition of a business process pattern 74
- 5.8.2 Business Process Pattern in Visual Paradigm 75
- 5.8.3 Complex Business Process Patterns – Example: Return of an Online Article 76
- 6 Methodology and Agility 78
  - 6.1 Project Charter 78
  - 6.2 Content, Presentations, Structure 79
  - 6.3 "Storytelling" - Collecting Information 80
  - 6.4 Relations in the Architecture 81
  - 6.4.1 Refinement 81
  - 6.4.2 Adding Details 81
  - 6.4.3 Logical Relations 82
  - 6.4.4 Relationships in Tools 82
  - 6.5 Structure - Classifications 82
  - 6.6 Architecture Principles, Style Guide, Model Policies, Model Governance 84
  - 6.7 Style Guide (Example) 87
  - 6.8 Model Policy (Example) 90
  - 6.9 Governance – Approvals, Maintenance 94
  - 6.9.1 Governance – Processes and Models 96
  - 6.9.2 Governance - Business Process Optimization and Business Process Improvement 98
  - 6.10 Roles in Model Development 99
- 7 Tools 102
- Part II: Blog-Posts and Short Essays 107
- 8 Visual Paradigm™ and Collaboration with Confluence ® 109
  - 8.1 Visual Paradigm™ 109
  - 8.2 Confluence and Visual Paradigm 110
  - 8.3 Manage the Media Break 114
  - 8.4 Summary 114
- 9 Separation of Concerns and Levels of Detail 115
  - 9.1 Introduction, Basic Architecture Principles 115
  - 9.2 Separation of Concerns and Architecture Frameworks 115
  - 9.3 Which abstractions do we choose? 116
  - 9.4 Several models in one abstraction 116
  - 9.5 Abstractions and Level of Detail 116
  - 9.6 Tool Support 118

10	Model Governance and Process Governance	119
	10.1 Scope	119
	10.2 Create, Use, Maintain Model – Model Governance	119
	10.2.1 Create Models	*119*
	10.2.2 Organizational Regulations	*120*
	10.3 Process Mining, Data Mining; Technical Solutions	120
	10.4 Design, Measure and Maintain Business Processes - Process Governance	120
	10.5 KPI	121
	10.6 Summary	122
11	Language-Based BPM	123
	11.1 What is the problem? The Model-Language-Gap	123
	11.2 Language based techniques in the Modeling Process	124
	11.3 Language-Based-BPM – Synchronizing Language Presentation and Visual Models	124
	11.4 Low-Code – Backend-First	125
Literature		126
12	Index	130
13	Tables	132
14	Figures	133

1 Model-Based Business Engineering

Models are omnipresent. They serve as base for building, analyzing, optimizing Business Processes, Business Decisions, IT Systems, and much more. Models support many working techniques in Business Analysis. How can we expect good results, if the base is wrong, ambiguous, not sufficient, or just not readable? How can we develop Business Processes or organizations systematically and for long term use if we do not know the relevant views?

Despite model development often don't get the needed acceptance. Questions as "Are you still drawing pictures, or do you manage already?" are raised. The need for professional and efficient model development is not recognized. Often a wrong understanding of models and missing methods are the reasons for this. The book describes our understanding of Model-Based Business Engineering.

Business Modeling is not Business Management. But without models, it is not possible to manage your business.

On the other end of the spectrum, we find self-appointed gurus promoting a single concept or notations as the silver bullet. Specific model elements or improvements of standard notations are discussed vehemently. Model-Based Business Engineering sees (standard) notations as an essential mean. Which standard, notations, and concepts are best suited, depends on the model subject, our project goals, and the involved stakeholders. Notations alone don't help. Single concepts bring only isolated improvements. We need multiple views for a successful business change. A suitable method is essential.

Model development got a bad reputation in some business areas over time. Too expensive, not goal-oriented enough, key stakeholders not addressed, unsystematically, not maintainable are some of the arguments. The root cause is a non-systematic and unplanned approach. That's why we emphasize the "engineering" part of the definition of Model-Based Business Engineering. Models need to be developed in a goal-oriented, planned, and repeatable way. We use proven techniques, learn from other disciplines, and apply soft-skills to ensure involvement of the stakeholders. We need to watch the effort to develop the models. I favor the DAD-approach (Ambler and Lines, Disciplined Agile Delivery: A Practitioner's Guide to Agile Software Delivery in the Enterprise 2012). It is more focused on software development. Many ideas are true for business model development too.

1.1 Model-Based ...

We talk of Model-Based Business Engineering, not of Model-Driven Development. Models are needed for many practical techniques in the scope of Business Process Management. But they are "only" important means to an end. The business problem "We don't have enough models." doesn't exist.

1.2 Why models?

A model describes a „subject of interest" before we develop or change it. They help us to measure the properties of the objects. The "thing" or better the subject of interest is a system or a process or a business capability or an entire organization. "If you can't describe it, you can't build it." arguments John Zachman. I add you can't maintain it too.

Describing the subject of interest gives us the opportunity to think and decide which properties it should have. The model contains not only information about the subject itself. It also includes data about design decisions, knowledge sources, and other information.

Models are base for definition and realization of Business Processes and other organizational aspects. They are particularly base for maintenance and ongoing development of these assets over a long period. This implies that the models need to be maintained and governed over the lifecycle of the object to keep model and reality in sync. Else the effort to create models is not justified.

1.2.1 What is a Model?

Customers or workshop attendees tell me sometimes that they don't use models. I'm sure that they do. They mean they don't use formal models. Models have very different forms and contents. Text, Tables, Story Boards, or MindMaps are models too. Everybody is using some type of models.

A model is an abstract description of a subject of interest. We highlight single properties of the subject. Which properties they contain depends on the subject, but even more on the project charter and the stakeholders addressed.

Models describe a few properties of the model subject especially, e.g., the flow of a Business Process or the responsibilities in a process or the risk of activities. Models describe complex interrelationships between single elements of the model elements too, e.g., a model of a Business Capability showing different aspects of the Capability in context.

Models come in different forms. Not all models are formal models using standard notations. Not all models are visual models. A table or a textual description can be a model. It is crucial to keep proven and successful description forms in an organization. Existing descriptions or description forms should be enhanced, improved, combining them with new formal notations.

1.2.2 Presenting Models - Formal (Standard-)Notations

We think of standard notations of the Object Management Group (OMG) as "Business Process Model and Notation" (BPMN) or "Decision Model and Notation" (DMN) first when talking about formal models.

Visual notations are the preferred form today. Many tools support the OMG standard notations. Standard exchange formats are available.

This is an advantage: the formal standard notations define not only a notation but also a standardized exchange format. These exchange formats allow the transfer of models between different modeling tools but also between the modeling environment and other applications, e.g., for simulation or reporting or measuring.

It is easier to conceive and understand a visual model. But a model is much more than a picture. The visual information is never complete. Much information about the model elements is hidden behind the image captured and stored in our model repository. The standard notations define a set of attributes for each model element. We can and should extend these attribute sets with additional properties we need for our project. The visualization shows one particular aspect of the subject of interest. The picture shows us this aspect and helps us to navigate and find other relevant information easily.

The description of the model elements contains more than the intrinsic attributes of the subject of interest (primary model content). It also includes information about design decisions, assumptions, restrictions, or knowledge sources (secondary model content).

1.2.3 Presenting Models - Informal Descriptions

Many informal presentation forms exist in addition to the standard notations. On one hand, they are often easier to use. At the same time, they sometimes lack tool support and exchangeability. Examples for such informal presentations are the "North Star Concept" by Roger Burlton of Process Renewal Group or the "Business Model Canvas" by Alexander Osterwalder (Alexander Osterwalder 2010). RACI-Charts are an addition to BPMN-descriptions. We find such descriptions mostly on higher levels of detail. As with the standard model notations, the visual (core) part is not very expressive and will be completed by other (secondary) information.

1.2.4 Language

Language is essential for all types of model presentation. Models are used to communicate between humans. Models are created from language. It should be possible to translate it back into language. For the visual part of the model, we define naming conventions. The detailed description of the elements always contains textual parts. The secondary information uses mainly language information. We need to understand the words used (see Introduction to SBVR – The Vocabulary)

Language offers a large degree of freedom to describe subjects. To avoid ambiguity and misunderstandings, regulated language specification is often used. We specify which content should be included. We give guidelines on how to develop and present details. E.g., we define a table format and ask for specific information. We came full circle: Combine proven presentations with new concepts.

Some content is presented textual only. An example is RueSpeak™ by Ron Ross – an approach to present business rules in natural language (Pitschke und Ross, RuleSpeak® Guidelines-Grundlagen, Version 1.2 2009).

1.2.5 Model and Model-Output

A common misconception in model development is that model and model output are seen as the same. That's wrong. Some modern web-based modeling tools amplify this misconception. This is not about how to access the model, but about specific content and different presentations for different stakeholder. The fact that everybody can access the model in the intranet/internet ignores the fact that we need different views, different content for different stakeholders. Model and Model Output have different target audiences and different goals. They overlap in some parts. The visual presentation is usually the link between both. The model must be rich enough to create the needed outputs.

Model	Model Output
Modeler is main stakeholder.	Different Stakeholder: Management, QA, Compliance Officer, Operator, Worker, …
Should be maintainable in an easy way and long term	Should be understandable; should comply with the user experience
Should be consistent	Should be adaptable to new views and formats
Focus on single views	Focus on a combination of different contents and views, compiled from different models
Must contain all information for the requested outputs	Different formats needed: HTML, PDF, MS Word, …
Should be evaluated and analyzed easily	Should be easy to find relevant information

Table 1: Model vs. Model Output different requirements

The model output addresses in form and contents our stakeholders first. Often the requested form doesn't allow easy maintenance. The different stakeholders require very different presentations and different content for the same model subject and the same level of detail. TOGAF defines the concept of View and Viewpoint. The different outputs need to be generated from the same model. The outputs don't define how we structure our models and the model repository.

The structure of Models and the Model Repository has to support maintenance, long term use, evaluation, and other requirements. The structure has to support model governance. Other issues as access rights and collaboration have to be taken into account.

The model output determines which content we need in our model repository. The question of stakeholders and their views is the start of the modeling effort.

1.3 Content, Comprehension, and Form of Presentation
1.3.1 What should be in a model? Primary and secondary Model content

A model should reflect all relevant views on the model subject. E.g. for a Business Process we are interested in the flow of activities, the details of each activity, the participants in the process, and their communication. To understand all this, we need additional information. E.g., What is the scope of the process? What assumptions did we have? Which information and which process context is given? We summarize these parts – content, assumptions, restrictions – as *Primary Model Content*.

To make sure the model is easy to understand and traceable, we need more information. This is not information about the model subject per se but results from the modeling and design process. These are knowledge sources and design decisions in the first row. This helps us to understand where the information in our models come from – maybe from a regulation or policy, perhaps from a stakeholder or a subject matter expert. This is essential information for maintenance, governance, and impact analysis of our models. During the design process, we make decisions. We prefer one option over another how the process or the capability should be built. What is in the scope? What is not? How do we plan the flow of activities? It is not only the result of the design decision, which is of interest. We have to understand the rationale behind such a decision. The reasoning behind is even more important than the result itself. Which goal has a higher priority than another?

Depending on the goals of our effort, more information is maybe needed. This information is for understanding our models and for governance essential too. Often this information is requested for the output by some stakeholders.

We summarize this group of information – knowledge sources, design decisions, other information – as *Secondary Model Content*.

At conferences or in social networks you hear or read the quote "All Models are wrong, some are useful.", coined to Georg Box. The quote always gets good applause. I don't like the quote. Georg Box was a statistician. He made the statement not really in the context of developing visual models, but in the context of statistics.

We invest effort and resources into developing our models. If the only reaction is "… is wrong anyway …" you feel a kind of tragedy. In any case, I try to create good models, created in a repeatable way, which are correct. We learn techniques. Notations and methods. This book is a try to pass such experiences. This is also the goal of the mentioned conferences.

I'm confident that our models are correct and valuable and useful. Correct doesn't mean "100% complete and a 100% reflection of reality" or "100% accurate in a mathematical sense". We highlight specific properties; we ignore other attributes, not important for our purpose.

It's not possible (and not sensible) to describe the reality of a subject 100% in a model. The specified attributes must support the purpose of our models (... some are useful ...). Sometimes esthetic considerations influence the design of our models. These restrictions and considerations (esthetics, culture, believes) are often not documented. Without documenting these reasons, we cannot asses the quality of the models.

That's why we collect this information as "Secondary Content" (see Figure 2: Primary and secondary Model content).

Be aware of your effort. We need to maintain our models. It makes more sense, to describe a Business process less detailed (incomplete?) but including the "Secondary Content". Defining the abstraction levels must consider this too (see Figure 7: Level of Detail (BCS-Framework).

We also need to define how we assess the quality of our models (Figure 10: Quality Criteria for Model Assessment). Maybe we declare some (primary and secondary) content mandatory.

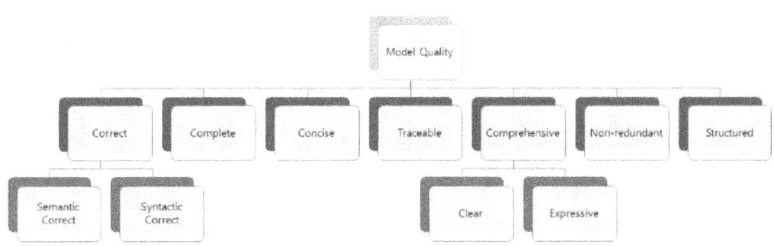

Figure 1: Quality Criteria for Models

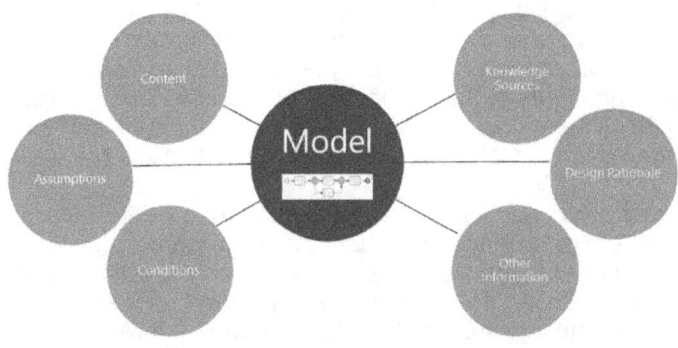

Figure 2: Primary and secondary Model content

1.3.2 Organize Primary Model Content

To achieve good maintenance for our model, we need a structured model repository. We follow the perspectives of the Zachman Framework for Enterprise Architecture. Model-Based-Business-Engineering focuses on the perspectives Scope and Business Concepts. We develop and describe requirements for the System Logic perspective too. Table 2: Typical model content in the perspectives of the Zachman Framework (Examples) shows examples of typical model content for these perspectives.

Perspective	Content
Scope / Contexts	Process Map, Capability Map, Vision, Goals, Objectives, Heat Maps
Business Concepts	Business Process Models, Decision Models, Business Capability Models, Business Requirements, Organizational Structure
System Logics	Requirements for IT and technology support

Table 2: Typical model content in the perspectives of the Zachman Framework (Examples)

1.3.3 Secondary Model Content

The value of a model is not only in the description of the primary model content of the subject of interest (see 1.3.1: What should be in a model? Primary and secondary Model content. The design decisions, restrictions or guidelines for the process or capability are equally important and sometimes even more. In our view, the secondary content is mandatory for a good model.

Elements or attributes for such information are not present in most standard notations as BPMN. The standard notation DMN defines the model element "Knowledge Source". It is explicitly shown and available for impact analysis and evaluation. We have to find own solutions if the notation we choose lacks such elements. Which options are available depends also on the tool used.

The rationale behind the design decisions is in the core of Business Process Management. We document the result and the reasoning for traceability and assessment.

1.4 ... Business ...
1.4.1 Business – What is the subject of interest?

The subject of interest in Model-Based Business Engineering is the enterprise. A good IT system or a single Business Process doesn't ensure a successful organization.

The purpose of our models is the development and improvement of "Business Capabilities".

„Business" has many facets. We need to address the different stakeholder views on different levels of detail. We need to be clear about vision, goals and strategy of the enterprise before we talk about operative business processes and business decisions. We are interested in the business process flow, responsibilities, supporting IT systems and other relevant information on the operational level. E.g., to improve processes in a warehouse, you need to know the topology of the warehouse. Therefore, we talk about "Business Capabilities". Figure 3: Burlton Hexagon to describe a Business Process Centric Capability Figure 3: Burlton Hexagon to describe a Business Process Centric Capability Figure 3 shows the Burlton Hexagon for describing process-centric Business Capabilities.

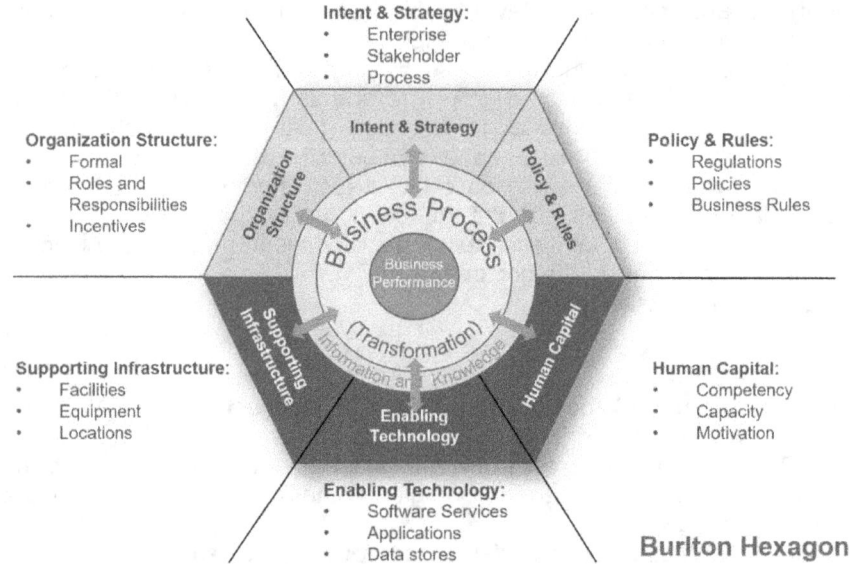

Figure 3: Burlton Hexagon to describe a Business Process Centric Capability

We need to specify the different information required, a structure for presenting the models, and a structure for the organization of the model repository. As said, we use the Zachman Framework for Enterprise Architecture as a base (The Zachman-Framework). Other frameworks and structures are possible. I will revisit the topic "Capability" later. The message here is that it is not enough to describe the business process in the narrower sense. The description of the context of the business process is also necessary.

1.4.2 Business and IT – What is the role of technology in Model-Based Business Engineering?

Business without IT or technology, in general, is not thinkable today. We discuss the "Internet of Things" or the digitization of Business Processes. Both include technical solutions as well as the business view.

IT has to be "business aware" the same way as business has to be "technology aware". Business and IT together need to evaluate the use of technologies for better business solutions solving business problems.

System descriptions, system requirements, relations between systems, and business capabilities are in the scope of Model-Based Business Engineering. Especially requirements for Business-IT-Systems are part of the approach. The development and description of systems are not in focus. Different model-based approaches exist for this as the Model-Based System Engineering (MBSE). We understand Model-Based Business Engineering as complementary to such methods.

1.5 ... Business Engineering – Develop Business Capabilities systematically

We understand model development for business as an engineering discipline. This means
- We can plan it.
- The quality of our models can be measured.
- Model development is comprehensible and repeatable.
- Models can be maintained and used long term.
- Design decisions are made with a reason.

This should be obvious but isn't so in daily practice. The request to produce models in a comprehensive and repeatable way causes discussions. We expect that the resulting models are comparable if they are based on the same information independently which team member created them. Modeling is a creative activity. The models will not be identical. We make different design decisions resulting in different models. That's why capturing this information is essential. If the result is entirely different, something is wrong, and we don't follow an engineering approach.

1.5.1 Standard-Notations, informal Descriptions, Styleguides

Standard Notations are essential to achieve the stated goals.

We experience many discussions about flaws and incompleteness of notation in social networks or at conferences. No question – all the standard notations leave room for improvements. But in most cases, they offer a better base compared to proprietary notations. They all include an extension mechanism to integrate additional attributes to cover own requirements and information needs. The defined exchange format allows to use different tools and to collaborate. All standard notations leave a (large?) degree of freedom to the modeler because they address very different usage scenarios. You have to ensure that everybody in the team has the same understanding of the concepts and the notation no matter if you use a standard notation or an own one. This includes developing a common view and understanding of the concepts but also rules how to use the elements of the notation. Such rules range from simple guidelines as using colors or naming model elements to more complex questions as using (or not using) specific elements and attributes or defining patterns to apply. Typically, we define a Style Guide or Modeling Wiki and a Modeling Guideline for our team.

1.5.2 Modeling and Working Techniques

Many practical techniques for capturing, analyzing, and transforming information into models exist. We use best practices for estimating and planning model projects. Working techniques include process mining, textual analysis, techniques for interviewing, workshop organization, facilitation, and many more.

Applying such techniques is essential part of Model-Based Business Engineering.

A good introduction into the topic "Facilitation" are the books by Ingrid Bens (Bens, Facilitating with Ease!: Core Skills for Facilitators, Team Leaders and Members, Managers , Consultants, and Trainers 2005) and (Bens, Facilitation at a Glance!: Your Pocket Guide to Facilitation (Memory Jogger) 2012)

Large parts are dedicated to the involvement of people in collecting information, designing and implementing Business Processes and Business Capabilities.

We need to involve the stakeholders in designing an enterprise. We create models, not as an end in itself.

1.6 Business Engineering is People Business

Our models support our business but are means to the end.

We need the engagement of our stakeholders in our effort to design and improve Business Capabilities. Our models need to support this.

The designed processes have to be implemented. Change Management is an outstanding discipline in Business Management. Change Management uses our models to communicate Business Processes, organizational structure, and planned changes.

Designing the model output requires a good understanding of the stakeholder, their requirements, expectations, and experiences.

This is strongly connected to the culture of the organization. Implementing Business Processes and Business Capabilities requires a specific culture and cultural change.

1.6.1 Continues Improvement and Model Governance

Business Engineering is not a one-time effort. Processes and capabilities need to be improved continuously to stay competitive. We monitor processes and measure key performance indicators based on our models. We change processes and capabilities based on these results.

Continuous improvement of Business Processes and the organizational context brings the danger that models and reality are no longer in sync after some time. We have to make sure both stay in sync or we risk to lose our investment in the models. We define Governance Rules and processes for the maintenance of our models.

1.7 Business Process Models and Structure

To achieve sustainable models, we need to answer two important questions:

- How do we design (structure) our (process-) models and which roles in the modeling process exist in our team?
- How do we organize the structure/architecture of our models?

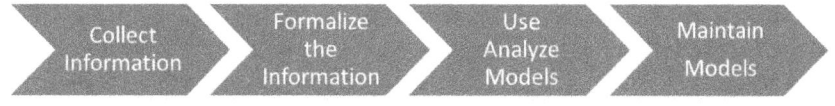

Facilitation Workshops; Questionnaires; MindMaps; Interviews; Observation;	Develop Models and Model Output Content;	Design Output – HTML, PDF, Word	Governance-Processes
User Stories; Story Boards; Forms;	Formal Standard Notations: BPMN, UML, BMM, SysML, SBVR, Archimate, Informal Descriptions: North Star-Concepts, IGOE	HeatMaps	
Facilitator, Interviewer	Process Modeler, Analyst, System Modeler	Writer, Analyst	

As we see in the previous overview, the standard notations like BPMN are not so important in all phases of the project. In the first phase, information must be collected, evaluated, and prioritized according to our project assignment. We have to define roles for our project team. This is not shown in the overview. Which project member perceive which responsibilities? Even if we choose an agile approach, not every employee is equally well suited for specific tasks. Scott Ambler mentions in the book (Ambler and Lines 2012) that in agile approaches very high specialization is not encouraged. This does not mean that there is no specialization and no role definitions. In this context, Ambler speaks of "Generalized Specialists". Too many skills are necessary, as a single individual employee master all of them (equally well). At the same time, the overall overview and understanding must be given. See 6.10: Roles in Model Development

1.8 Structure, Structure, Structure

In any case, in all phases of model development finding a good model structure is an essential technique for the development and maintenance of our repositories and the individual models (see 6.5: Structure - Classifications). Therefore, not only modeling notations are presented in the book (see Section 5.3: "Describing Business Processes – CMMN").

Independent of the used description form (Standard Notation, informal description) we need to know the rules of the used presentation. Which objects may be related? In any case, the question of structuring is essential for collecting the information, development, maintenance, and evaluation of the models. In the next chapter, you'll learn about the architecture framework I use (Zachman Framework ™ for enterprise architecture) and the detail levels named in 2.2: Detail Level in my projects.

2 The Zachman-Framework for Enterprise Architecture™

As emphasized, we need an architecture (structure) to organize our model elements. If the company is part of our project, we need a structure that helps us to present the relevant views of the company and the relationships between the views. Our modeling approach uses the Zachman framework for this. The Zachman framework (Zachman 2001) is an architectural pattern represented by a matrix. It defines different perspectives (lines) and different abstractions in each perspective (columns). The subject of the framework is the entire company. **Fehler! Verweisquelle konnte nicht gefunden werden.** shows the Zachman Framework™.

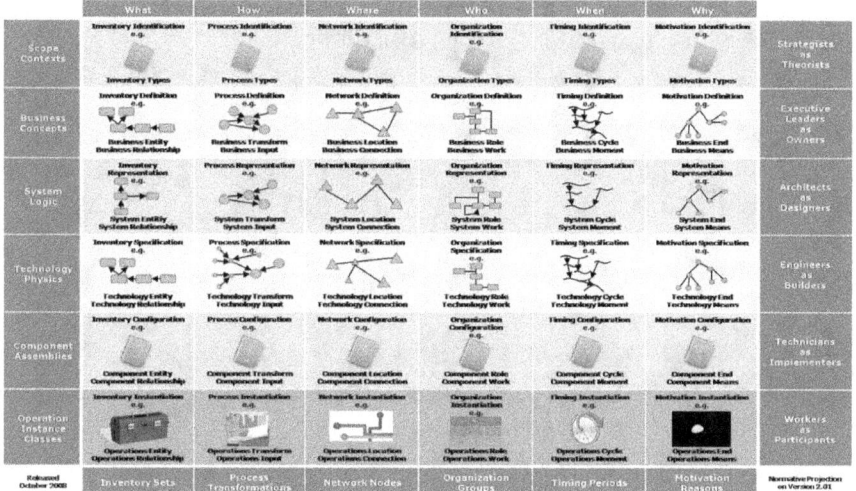

Figure 4: The Zachman Framework™

We find other frameworks in literature and theory (TOGAF, NAF, DoDAF) or proprietary frameworks (such as the Qualiware EA Framework, see Figure 5: The Qualiware EA Framework). All of these frameworks follow the same basic principle and can often be mapped to each other. For our projects, we chose the Zachman Framework because it is method-neutral (unlike TOGAF) and is supported by several tools (Visual Paradigm, MagicDraw, Qualiware). The proprietary frameworks are often associated with modeling tools too. Since the basic principles are comparable and can be mapped to each other, a dispute over "the best framework" is not worthwhile.

More important, it is to find an architecture (structure) for our models (for the structure of our repository). Structuring is a very important skill. In my view, the ability to structure the repository and the models is more important than mastering different notations such as BPMN or CMMN.

The knowledge of the notations and the underlying principles is important in order to find a suitable structuring.

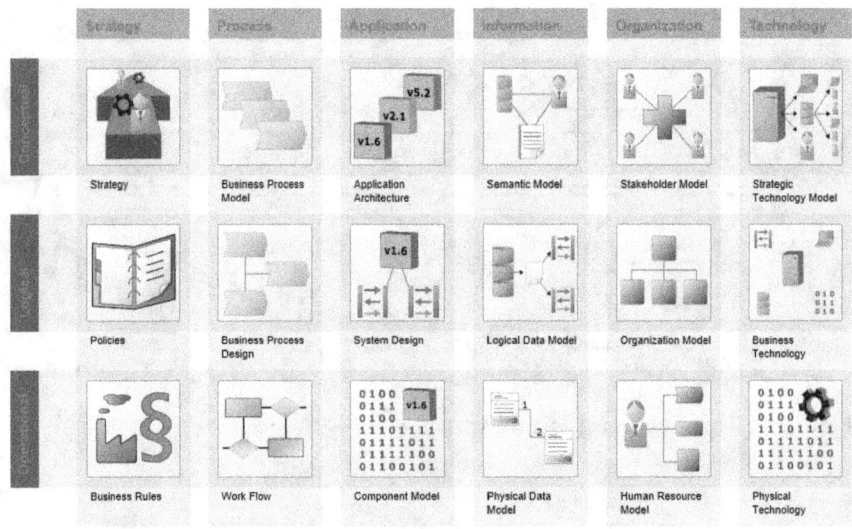

Figure 5: The Qualiware EA Framework

None of the mentioned frameworks speaks of the various Detail level required. Zachman only speaks of the need for detail level. We do not represent a business process on just one detail level. We usually follow a top-down approach. We start with a "process map" that only names the business processes and frames the general top-level business processes. Based on this, we present more detailed models down to the task level.

There are connections between perspectives and details. Within a perspective there are close connections between the individual abstractions.

Even within an abstraction, there are relations: the fact model, for example, is a prerequisite for the logical data model, which in turn is a prerequisite for the physical data model.

2.1 Content in the Zachman-Framework

Talking about a Business Model, we are talking about a composite model that includes single models in multiple perspectives, views, and detail level in the Zachman framework.

The "Business Model" includes all individual models of the perspective "Business Concepts" needed to realize ad measure to fulfill the project charter.

The term "Fachmodell", often used in German, includes individual models from the perspectives "Scope" and "Business Concepts". A system model for an IT system includes different models from the perspectives "System Logic" and "Technology Physics".

Table 2: Simple Models and Artifacts in the Zachman Framework™ labels commonly used model types and artifacts to the individual cells of the Zachman framework.

The table gives only an idea, which artifacts are often created for the respective view and does not claim completeness.

	What?	How?	Where?	Who?	When?	Why?
Scope		Process Map Process House				Vision /Mission
Business Concepts	Fact model/ Vocabulary Rule model	Process Model Activity Modell	Distribution Model (functional)	Organizatio nal Chart Role Model	Mile Stones	Business Requiremen ts
System Logic	Logical Data Model	Function Model Programm- design	Distribution Model (technical)	Role Mode (System Roles)	State Machines	Design Requiremen ts
Technology Physics	Physical Data Model	Impl. Model	Distribution Model (physical)	System User	System Dynamic	System Requiremen ts
Components Assemblies	Database- Structure	Programm Code	Network- specification	LDAP Directory		System Monitoring

Table 3: Simple Models and Artifacts in the Zachman Framework

For the representation of the contents, various standard notations and means of description are used. For the use of the notations and descriptions, not only the used framework is crucial, but also the selected level of detail.

For the same artifact, there are often several means of description available. A business process model can be presented using the BPMN standard but also using event-driven process chains or informal swimlane diagrams. At the same time, a notation can be used to represent different contents. For example, The UML class diagram can be used to visualize a fact mode., It can also illustrate the structure of an object-oriented program.

Which notation we use to represent some content depends on various questions. Can the desired content be displayed? Is the used tool supporting the notation? Do I have enough knowledge to apply the

25

notation? Does the receiver of the model (the stakeholder) accept the presentation? Is the model maintainable over a long period? Do the costs of the model justify the benefits?

The selected framework also helps us to structure the repository of the respective modeling tool. For example, if we choose a TOGAF project (a project that follows the TOGAF framework and the ADM (Architecture Development Method)), we not only get guidance on using the ADM, but the repository is automatically structured accordingly. See Figure 6: Using TOGAF ADM® in NoMagic.

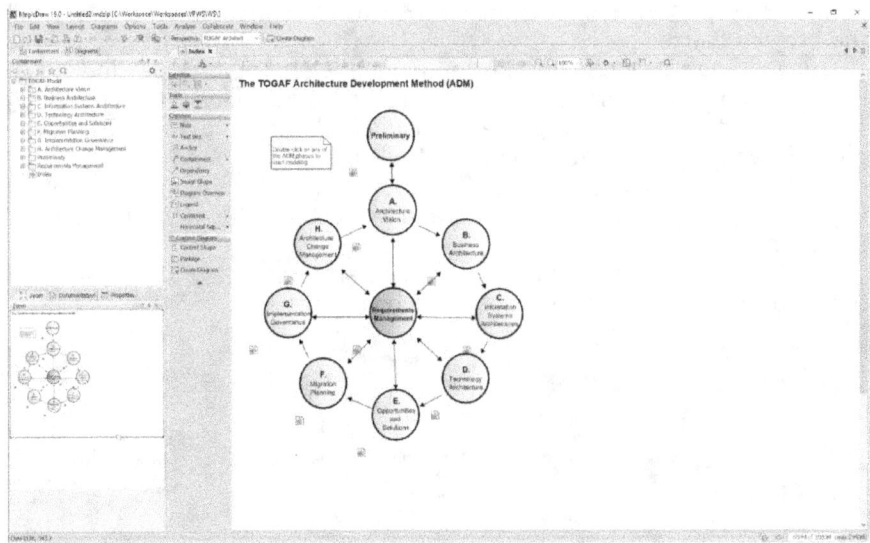

Figure 6: Using TOGAF ADM® in NoMagic

In addition to structuring the actual (primary) content (by framework and method), I always recommend my clients to create an area that is reserved for analyses and reports (for example, Where do we place a RACI chart?). An area for experiments is also recommended. We do not expect to know always immediately the right or optimal model solution. We have to experiment first.

The contents of each abstraction and level of detail determine which notation is most appropriate. Some standard notations are used in different perspectives. For example, BPMN is used both for the Business description of business processes (perspective "Business Concepts") and for the technical implementation (for example through a workflow engine, perspective "System Logic"). The fact that we use the same notation for both perspectives does not make any of the perspectives obsolete. The mapping from one perspective to the other is made easier. I don't agree to the statement by Smith and Fingar in (Howard Smith 2006)) "Do not bridge the business IT divide - Obliterate it.". (BPMN 2.0 2010) therefor defines "Conformance Level" depending on the usage in one of the perspectives.

2.2 Detail Level

Even though the frameworks don't define the required detail level, this is an important question frequently asked by users. In our projects, we name the following detail level:

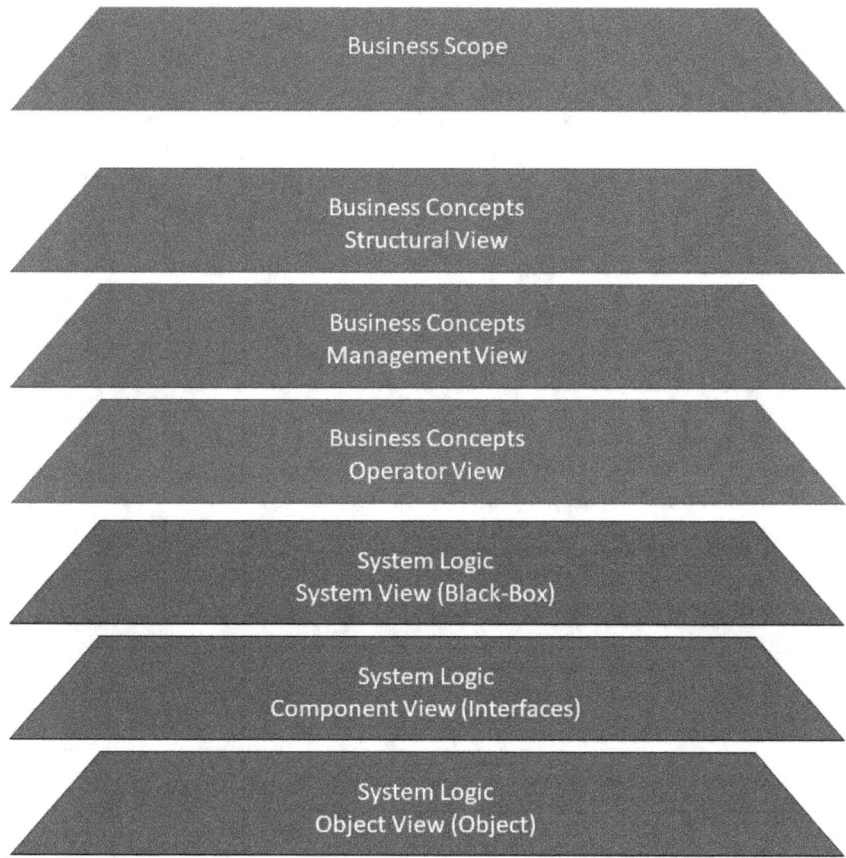

Figure 7: Level of Detail (BCS-Framework)

At workshops, I always emphasize that the magic number is "three." Whether this system suits you or is too detailed depends on your project. So maybe you already need several levels of abstraction in the "Business Scope" perspective.
For us, the system shown in Figure 7 works well. In addition to the abstraction and purpose of the particular level of detail, we name typical stakeholders, the planned scope of the models, and the model elements used therein. This consideration helps us to decide on the notation elements used and possibly additionally required means of description.

The naming of the purpose of the detail level is better than a - often found - pure numbering (Level 1, 2, 3).

In the "Business Scope" perspective, we typically find the so-called process map (or process house). The purpose is the naming of the existing processes in the company, which will be described later in more detail. We name the processes first in the process map (scope) and refine the process through general sub-processes in the structural view. That is, we name the sub-processes of the respective overall process from a very general point of view, we structure and define boundaries. We find in our process map, e.g., the process "sea freight import". This process consists of different sub-processes: "carry out land transport" (the goods are transported to the ship), "carry out sea transport" (the goods are transported by ship), "plan transport" (the entire transport chain must be planned) , "Customs and Taxes" (the goods must be taxed at import/export), "Documentation" (the customer is informed about the steps taken) and "Make Billing" (we also have to earn money). For example, BPMN rarely plays a role in the process map. The processes are named and described informally. As a description tool, we often use a so-called "process map" (an informal notation without a standard). We also find, e.g., tabular representations too. In addition to naming the processes and classifying the business processes, general information about the business process is captured. What does the business process involve? What not (negative definition of the boundaries)? In addition to the form of presentation, we make specifications for cardinality. In the structural level, less than ten sub-processes of the overall process should be specified. The structural level uses "storyboards" often.

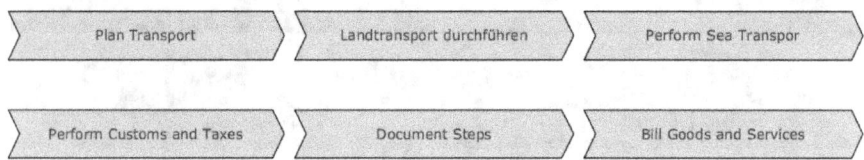

Figure 8: Structural Level of Business Process "Seafreight Import"

In the management view, we describe the sub-processes defined at the structural level in more detail. We describe the process from the point of view of a person, who want to understand the process, but does not need to know every detail and exception. "Management view" is not the best name. Even employees outside the management need this view. In addition to the process manager, these are often quality officers, employees responsible for ISO certification, or risk officers. Typically, BPMN is used here as a notation form. However, we do not use all the elements of BPMN and supplement these with other means of description. Sub-processes are mainly used to understand the process. Whether we already use pool and lanes at this level to describe responsibilities depends on the project. Gateways are used sparingly. First, we will illustrate the process through the "happy-day scenario". What is the intended "normal" process? Critical alternatives, options, and parallel activities are shown only. We give recommendations for the cardinality again. A sub-process scoped in the structural level should be refined into maximum 15 sub-processes.

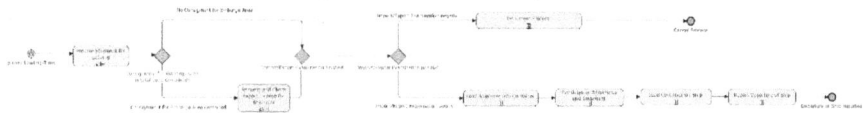

Figure 9: Management Level of process "Seafreight import"

From an operational point of view, we then describe the subprocesses of the management level in detail in the next level of detail level. We describe the processes for an employee who lives the process every day. We use BPMN again and supplement other means of description. The use of BPMN is limited. Since this level is no longer to be refined, only task and no sub-processes are used to describe the activities. Pool and lane are used at this level, complemented by the RACI concept. Each sub-process from the management point of view is subdivided into a maximum of 15 tasks. Exceptions and special cases are shown.

Whether we have to represent every abstraction and every level of detail for each process is a project-dependent decision. Scott Ambler (Ambler and Lines 2012) warns to develop models in great detail very early in the process cycle. The term "undermodel" is coined to Scott Ambler in this context. My experience is also that business processes are modeled to early, very quickly and in (too) great detail.

If we consider an overall process across all levels of detail, we present it by 10 x 15 x 15 = 2.250 activities. For most processes, that should be sufficient. Do you want to describe a process by more than 2.250 activities?

The abstractions and the level of detail helps us too using the models and to support a top-down approach for planning, defining priorities, and alike.

2.3   What is the purpose of a Model?

A good model serves one specific purpose - and preferably only one! If we need multiple purposes, we create several models and connect individual models and elements.

Models in the perspectives "System Logic" and "Technology Physics" are used not only to communicate properties of the system but also to create system components. UML class diagrams can be used to generate Java source code, ER diagrams to develop database structures or BPMN diagrams to provide workflow engines with control information.

To succeed, the model must meet various formal requirements. Such considerations often drive the discussion about models and the use of standard notations. If the model is formally wrong, the Java source code cannot be generated. However, a look into practice shows a different picture. Scott Ambler found in a survey that the majority of project teams do not use models for the automatic generation of system components, but for the documentation of system, design, requirements, etc.[1]

Whether the sample is representative, is an open question. However, my experience shows a similar distribution pattern in my customer base. If we ask the question in business process modeling, the percentages for generated system components are likely to be even lower. This doesn't mean that the generation of system components from models is unimportant. As more technology develops, the more often this question is asked. Modern workflow engines are easier and more convenient to use than five years ago.

Nevertheless, the generation of system components is only one aspect and dependents heavily on the project. What is the main purpose of our models? The answers from users to it are many. These range from "system documentation", "system design", "process documentation", "process analysis", "process optimization", "description of requirements" to "creation of invitations to tender" or "creation of work instructions" to "ISO certification". If we question these aspects, we find that there is an important aspect of it:

Models are used for communication!

Models are used for communication between different stakeholders. They are an essential communication tool. Business models first serve to communicate between different model users (stakeholders). The value is often seen in the mindset for creating the models. The models serve to communicate between business users or between business users and IT specialists. This will not change for the "Business Concepts" perspective - here, communication is the primary purpose to enable analysis, optimization, or requirement definition. Scott Ambler says: "The value of models is that "Model design gives us time to think"."

If we accept that models serve communication first, various discussions quickly become relative. For communication to succeed, the "recipient" or "reader" needs to understand the model. Thus, the criterion of "formal correctness" is less important compared to the criterion of "intelligibility". See Figure 38: Use of a Complex Gateway (Example, Visual Paradigm) for an example to avoid a notation element to avoid ambiguity. But of course, formal correctness is essential. The communication should not only be in an understandable form, but also avoid misunderstandings and allow a translation into a formal model. When we have to strike a balance between "intelligibility" and "formal correctness," intelligibility is more important. We comment model elements to support intelligibility and later formalization. The criterion "intelligibility" also requires the creation of a "vocabulary" containing the terms and definitions used (see chapter 4: Introduction to SBVR - The Vocabulary).

The question which model elements from the standard notations such as UML and BPMN are used changes the direction too: It is not important to use every element and to use every possibility of the

---

[1] Results from Scott Ambler's July 2008 Modeling and Documentation Survey posted at www.agilemodeling.com/surveys/

standard notation. This only makes sense if the receiver of the model is able to understand these elements as well (with the same meaning as we) and to use them in terms of communication. A "style guide" (How do we use the notation? What elements do we use? What are the naming conventions we use for models and model elements? How do we support the reader with further aids, such as legends?) is essential and highly suggested. (see 6.7: Style Guide (Example))

We need quality criteria to assess created models. We have already mentioned two criteria: "correctness" and "comprehensibility". One goal in the choice of model representations is to address both requirements equally.

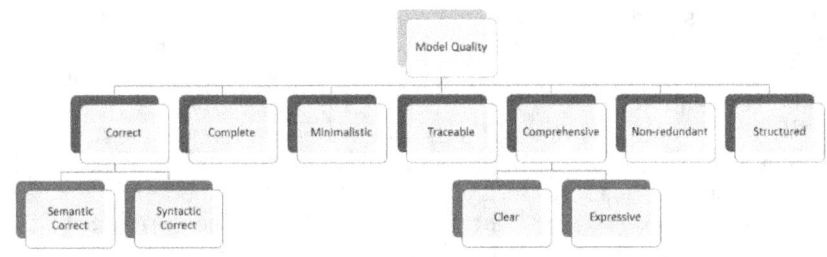

Figure 10: Quality Criteria for Model Assessment

Also, in relation to select modeling tools, new questions and criteria arise: What functions exist to support "communication"? Is it easy to generate different outputs? The spectrum ranges from published models in the intranet, creation of work instructions, preparation of evaluations, standard reports to formal and legally binding documents such as a call for tenders. What formats are supported for automatic output generation?

2.4 Notations for Enterprise Modeling

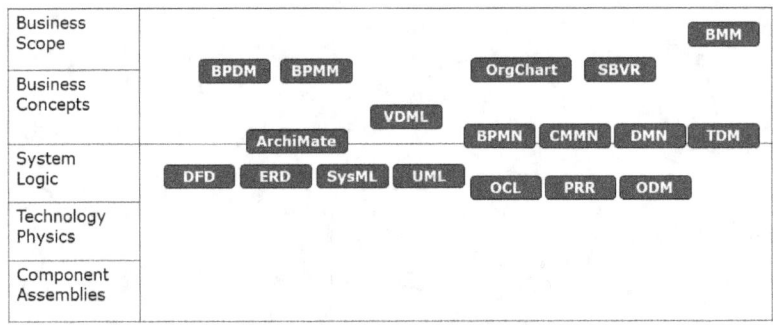

Figure 11: Notations for Enterprise Models

As a standardization body, the "Object Management Group" (OMG) has published a good number of standard notations for corporate modeling in recent years.

Other organizations (such as The OPEN Group) and companies have published notations too (sometimes as standard notation, sometimes proprietary, sometimes competing).

Each of the standards addresses a specific area of enterprise modeling, and each notation has pros and cons. The application of a single standard notation is always an isolated solution. At the same time, every standard notation tries to support different use cases and therefore leaves degrees of freedom. You (as a project team) have to specify the use of the standard notation. A good example is the use of the complex gateway in BPMN. The complex gateway often leads to misunderstandings. That's the reason that they are "forbidden" to use often. Again a "Style Guide" specifies such internal policies for Business Process Modell development.

We always have to be clear about the purpose of used standard notations.

Frequently, standards are evaluated and used from the view of IT. Part of the standards exclusively addresses the business view without considering the implementation in IT systems. Some models describe the relationships between the business and the IT view (for example, which system function supports which business activity?). Figure 11: Notations for Enterprise Models names a variety of known notations - whether formal standard notation or informal, proprietary notation.

Some standard notations used are briefly characterized.

BMM (Business Motivation Model) (BMM 2010)

BMM defines concepts such as "Vision" and "Mission", "Goals" and "Targets", "Influencer" and "Assessment". BMM is not a visual notation even if the elements are graphically visualized in some tools. First, it's about understanding the (motivational) concepts.

Semantics of Business Vocabulary and Rules (SBVR) and RuleSpeak

The standard (SBVR 2008) defines the elements of a business vocabulary and the definition of business rules. This is not about the definition of a graphic notation, but about the description of the concepts. For example, the standard is implemented by RuleSpeak. The English version of RuleSpeak is included as a reference in the appendix of the standard. You can find the German version on my website.

A defined vocabulary is a requirement for other models. Without a clear conceptual base, we build on sand. A good introduction to business vocabulary and business rule management (Ross 2009).

Business Process Model and Notation (BPMN)

BPMN (BPMN 2.0 2010) is the standard for describing (well-structured, predictable) business processes. The focus is on the description of the process flow and the communication between process participants. To understand the basic principles of BPMN (Allweyer 2009) is recommended. The BPMN is complemented by other concepts such as the IGOE concept (see (IDEF0 1993) and (Burlton 2001).

Case Management Model and Notation (CMMN)

Like BPMN, CMMN is intended to describe business processes. In contrast to the BPMN, especially for business processes that are not well predictable, but are designed according to the situation. We describe a plan for the realization of the process. Examples are the reclamation of orders, the failure of a loan, or the treatment of a patient.

Each company has both processes that are well represented by BPMN. As well as business processes, which are not easily modeled using BPMN and which are better described with CMMN.

The literature for CMMN is, unfortunately (still?) not very extensive. The specification of the standard can be found on the OMG website (CMMN 1.1 December 2016).

Decision Management Model (DMN) - (DMN 1.2 2019)
The Decision Model (TDM) - (Barbara von Halle 2009)
Semantics of Business Vocabulary and Rules (SBVR 2008)

Business processes include operational decisions. These are sometimes represented textually. An example is RuleSpeak (Pitschke and Ross, RuleSpeak Sentence Forms, Business Rules in Naturally German, Version 1.2 2009, Pitschke and Ross, RuleSpeak® Guidelines Fundamentals, Version 1.2 2009) that follows the SBVR standard (SBVR 2008). The disadvantage of SBVR is that it includes not a defined structuring principle. The result is the famous, extensive Rule Books.

DMN and TDM overcome the problem by structuring in multi-levels. We begin with naming the decisions contained in the business process or otherwise identified, name the needed sub-decisions and inputs, and define the relevant rules in a decision table. All business rules contribute to the named decision. We can start with individual decisions that are important to us and do not have to construct large rule bases first. If we use RuleSpeak™, we need a similar structuring criterion. The DMN and TDM approach is a top-down approach (from the decisions in the business process, the sub-decisions, and inputs, to the business rules used in the decision). A top-down approach supports planning and prioritization.

Figure 12: DMN Example (Qualiware) and Figure 13: TDM Example (Qualiware) show the same simple decision model in DMN and TDM (tool Qualiware). DMN is a defined OMG standard notation. TDM is a proprietary notation ((Barbara von Halle 2009)) supported by different tools. The decision which notation we prefer in our project depends on subjective factors too.

Beyond the visual notation, Barbara von Halle and Larry Goldberg (Barbara von Halle 2009) define principles for developing decision models and decision tables. These principles can also be used together with DMN. DMN contains additional elements (such as the Knowledge Source element) that TDM lacks. TDM is named "DMN compliant".

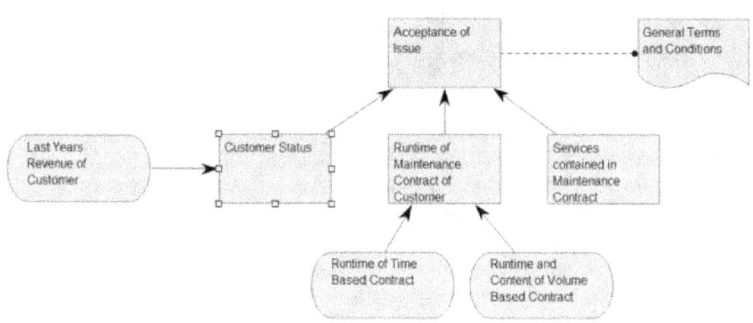

Figure 12: DMN Example (Qualiware)

The literature on decision modeling is extensive now. For DMN, I recommend the book by James Taylor and Jan Purchase (James Taylor 2016) and the OMG specification (DMN 1.2 2019). For TDM, the book by Barbara von Halle and Larry Goldberg (Barbara von Halle 2009) is the primary source. The available tool palette is extensive for both notations. Different tools support both notations and leave the choice to the user. Choice is always good.

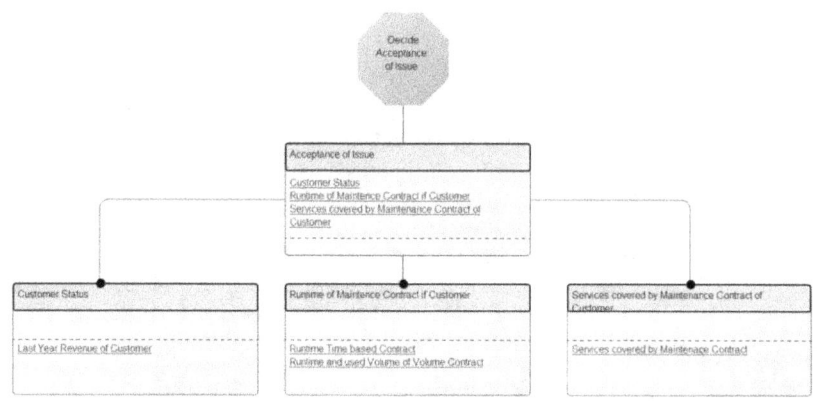

Figure 13: TDM Example (Qualiware)

Value Delivery Modeling Language (VDML) (Object Managment Group 2018)

Value Stream Models are an old and popular technic. In addition to the description of the activities on a large scale, the interaction of Roles (Collaboration) is important. The standard also addresses techniques as heatmaps. Tools do not necessarily use the standard but proprietary representations (see also 3: Process Maps, Process Houses and other overviews).

Unified Modeling Language (UML)

UML (UML 2010) is the standard notation for describing object-oriented IT systems. In fact, UML is a collection of 13 notations that describe the structural and dynamic aspects of an IT system.

We can also use individual parts of the UML, such as the class diagram, for business modeling. In this case we ignore all the properties and details that are implementation-specific.

When we use individual UML diagram types for business modeling, we must always be aware that UML has been developed for the description and implementation of object-oriented systems. In many places, the programming grins at us from below. We need to question the used model types.

The UML literature is very diverse (for example (Booch, Rumbaugh und Jacobson 2005), (Rupp, Queins und Zengler, UML 2 glasklar. Praxiswissen für die UML-Modellierung 2007)).

System Modeling Language (SysML)

The SysML (SysML 2010) is an extension of the UML. It includes the UML diagrams such as use case diagram, class diagram, etc. The SysML also includes a new diagram type, the requirements diagram.

The representation and systematization of requirements is essential for every project. We also use requirement diagrams in business process modelling

Of course, there was a life before the current standard notations of the OMG. Many of the standard notations emerged from previously existing notations. An example is the state machine diagram of the UML.

Even outside the standard notations, the "old" notations are still popular depending on the task. For example, the CRC-Cards (Class-Responsibility-Collaboration-Diagram) diagram (Wilkinson 1997). CRC cards are popular with developers in the early stages of SW development. Another popular notation is the Data Flow Diagram (DeMarco 1979). Beside the OMG-standards standard notations exist originated by other standard organizations.

The Opengroup AchiMate ® 3.0

An example is Archimate® by the Opengroup. The elements are already assigned to the respective perspective in the architecture. (See The Zachman-Framework). Archimate is supported by several tools, as it is particularly well-suited for linking different views. Questions as "Which business processes support which goal?" Or "Which systems support which business processes?" can be answered and presented well in Archimate.

Data Flow Diagram

Data flow diagrams as described in (DeMarco 1979) is an old, non-standard form of presentation that has recently gained in popularity. It not only defines the (graphical) form of presentation, but also provides methodological guidance. Especially in the context of the GDPR, data flow diagrams are well suited to illustrate the relationship between business processes and the data used. This information can also be presented in Archimate®. The popularity of DFDs results from the fact that DFDs being limited to one (or a few) views. DFD answers the question which data are used in which processes. Where do these data come from, where do they go to? Using the standard extension mechanisms of the modeling tools, we collect additional (primary and secondary) information that is relevant to our project assignment. In the context of GDPR, for example, this includes information on the confidentiality of the data. In addition to the alternative representation in Archimate®, it is also possible to describe and analyze the relationships between business processes (e.g. described by means of BPMN) and the data used (described by ERD or UML diagrams) by the feature of establishing relationships between model and model elements available in the modeling tools (see 6.4: "Relations in the Architecture"). Which option seems most appropriate depends on the project assignment and our stakeholders.

Virtually all tools allow linking different models and individual model elements to track the relationships and their evaluation without the use of Archimate. Once we decided on the notations and features to use, we need to bring all members of our team up to speed in using the notation, the tool and features (e.g., for linking elements). Therefore, we define training, a style guide and a modeling policy for our enterprise.

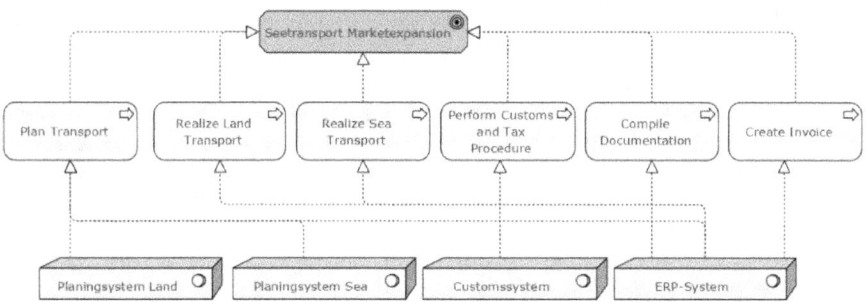

Figure 14: Example ArchiMate (Visual Paradigm)

In projects, we use further means of description. Not all are formally standardized but commonly used. Some methods of presentation are de facto standards. Examples are mind maps, organization charts, process maps or even the known "Story Boards". In any case, you have to deal with the respective (standard) notation before applying it. And you need to understand the concepts - whether formal standard notation or not.

In addition to the visual representations, we always use textual and tabular descriptions. Some methods use tabular representations very intense. Considerations such as the necessary effort and the acceptance by the stakeholders are crucial.

It is not the aim of this book to fully depict individual notations. Notations and elements are described as needed. If interested, you will find open workshops for different notations on our website. Please refer to the relevant literature and my previous book (J. Pitschke, Unternehmensmodellierung für die Praxis: Band 1: Eine Einführung in die Darstellung von Unternehmensmodellen 2011), which focused on the presentation of models through standard notations. The content should not be repeated here, but some new standard notations and developments appeared and are explained and discussed.

I already pointed out that a single perspective or a single view is not enough. For a business model, we need to describe multiple views, including the relationships between those views.

Are all views equally important? And with what view do we start our modeling project? Our approach is a process-oriented approach. That means business process models are a central element for our business models. But that does not necessarily mean that we look at processes first. It just means that business process models are central and connecting elements of our consideration.

Business processes as a central element to enterprise modeling is not new knowledge. The discussion has been going on for many years through the literature (e.g., (Rummler und Brache 1995)). For more information and suggestions on business process management, see (Tregear, Reimagining Management 2018).

Individual questions are illustrated with examples of different descriptions and notations created with various tools (Qualiware, Visual Paradigm, MagicDraw).

For examples and discussions, we consider an imaginary company "FatBuddha". It is an Israeli (fictitious) brewery specializing in craft beer. FatBuddha's CEO has assigned us to assist his team in the enterprise description (business architecture) with a particular focus on business process modeling. The FatBuddha team has little or no modeling experience so far.

As a first aid measure, employees are trained in the use of individual means of description and notations (including BPMN) and in various working techniques. In particular, the aim is to structure existing models and make them usable.

3 Process Maps, Process Houses and other overviews

The first question is: which processes do we consider? We define the scope of our project. We can also refer to tabular representations. Frequently, however, simple visual representations are selected, for example so-called "process maps" or "process overviews". Process maps are a popular, non-standard form of presentation.

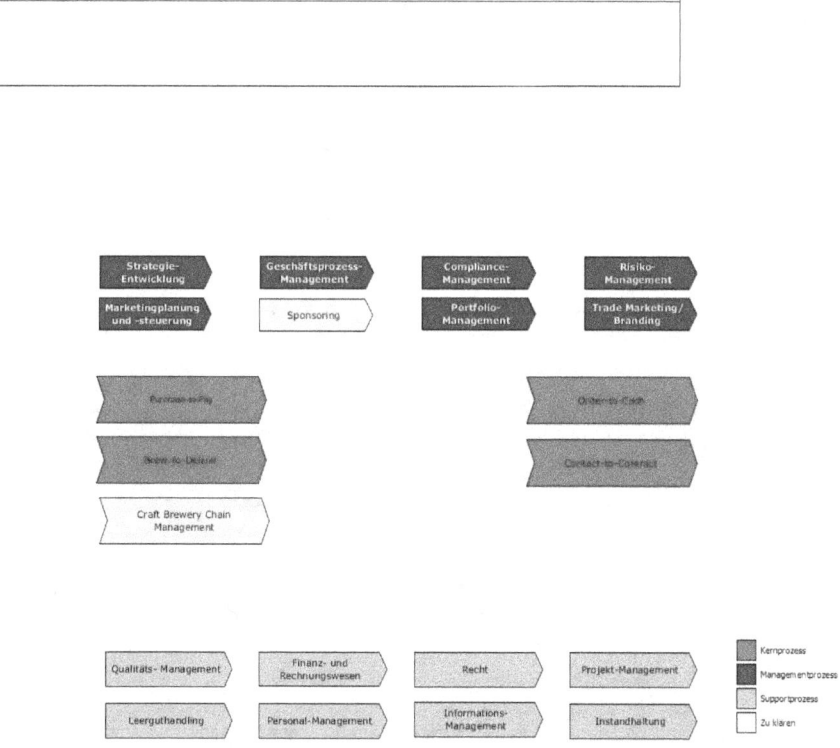

Figure 15: Sample Process House Fat Buddha (Visual Paradigm)

In addition to the representation by the ProcessMap or tabular forms, value stream diagrams are quite popular in the moment. There is even a formal OMG standard (Object Managment Group 2018). Modeling tools support these notations or proprietary representations. Value models are more detailed and contain more information than ProcessMaps. It is essential that activities are presented globally (in general). A more detailed presentation is done on the management level and on the operator level using BPMN connected with additional descriptions. The name of this perspective is "Scope". So the intention is to name the business processes, to scope them (What is inside? What is outside), and to describe them in a general way.

Value stream models are used at the structural level too as a substitute for process overviews / process maps.

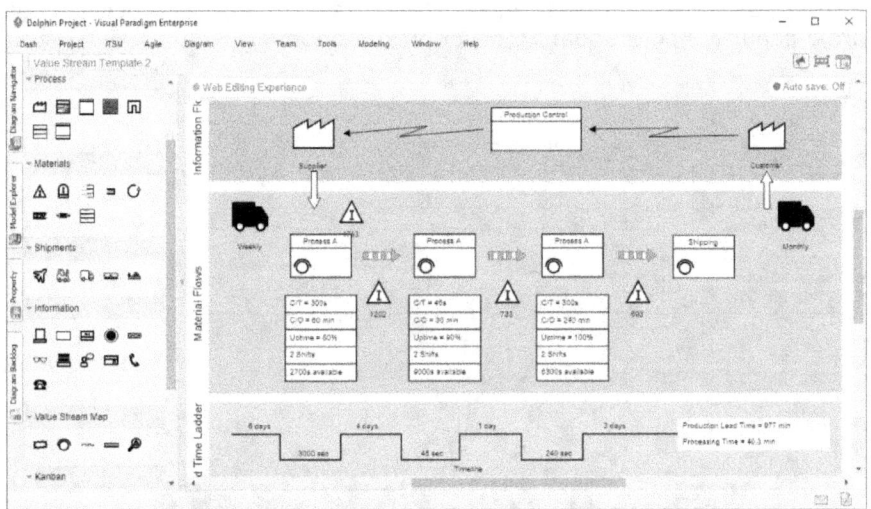

Figure 16: Value Delivery Model (Source Visual Paradigm)

In addition to naming the processes, there is a need for further description, prioritization and classification. Processes are classified as "core processes", "management processes", and "support processes". In addition to the tabular classification; we use color representations and legends. Figure 15: Sample Process House Fat Buddha (Visual Paradigm)

The main goal of such process maps or process houses is to name and scope the processes. In the example above, we see the process "sponsoring". Should this process be part of the standard marketing process? Or is this really an independent process? There is no right or wrong in such questions. It is essential to clarify these questions and to record the decisions and decision criteria (see paragraph 1.3.1).

We need to understand what we mean by a core process, what under a management process, what is a support process, and how to apply the criteria consistently in the team.

In addition to scope the business processes, we want to attract attention of the stakeholders to our business process models. Textual descriptions are used. Techniques are helpful. E.g., we create so-called "Story Boards" which can be used not only to scope the business processes but also to prioritize them. Which processes are more important to us? In which order do we want to look into them? Which depend on each other or are otherwise related? A good source for "story boards" is (Martin Sykes 2012). Story Boards are also used in Agile Modeling a lot.

3.1 Motivational Elements

It is recommended at the beginning of the project do dispute the vision and goals, in short, the motivation of the enterprise. If we want to describe the elements formally, it is worth taking a look at BMM (BMM 2010). In addition to this formal presentation, there are many informal descriptions of the motivational elements. In (Burlton 2001) Roger Burlton describes the "North Star" concept as a motivational element. Here are many similar concepts. The mentioned story boards give us information about the motivation of the enterprise and the prioritization too.

Since there exist a good number of concepts, many tools have their own way to describe and prioritize the motivation.

3.2 Business Motivation Model

No matter which representation we choose, we need the information for the design, prioritization, and evaluation of our models. BMM defines the following elements: "Means" and "Ends". Means are used to achieve an end. The accessibility of an end and the choice of means depend on various influencing factors (influencers) and their assessment (assessment). Figure 16: Overview BMM shows the elements.

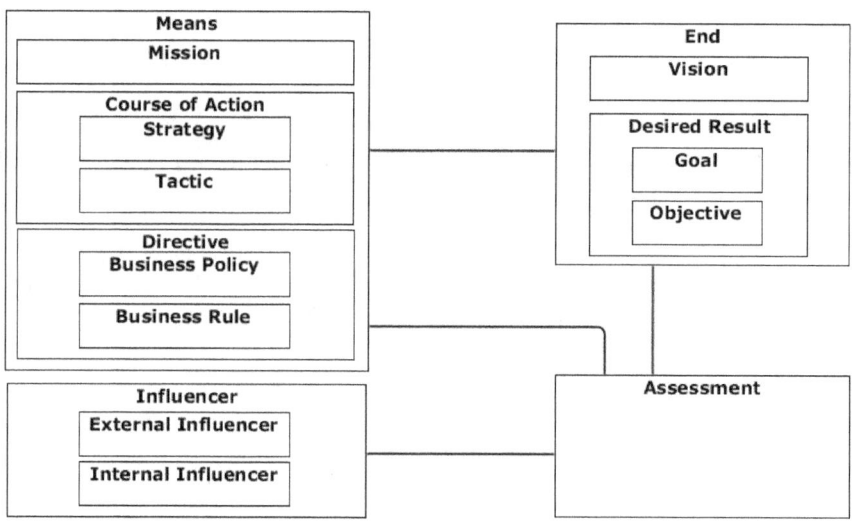

Figure 17: Overview of BMM

A vision (Ends) describes what a company wants to be, what position it wants to take in the market or how it wants to be perceived by customers.

The vision generally describes what a business wants to be or become.

41

Desired results are more specific than the vision. A Goal is more likely to be long-term, and the objective is more qualitative than quantitative. A goal must be precise enough to derive goals.

Objectives describe individual steps to be achieved on the way to the goal. A goal has a defined date. For a goal, we define criteria that allow to measure if the goal has been achieved. Means describe what we do to achieve our goals. Figure 17: Motivation FatBuddha gives an example of the use of the BMM standard.

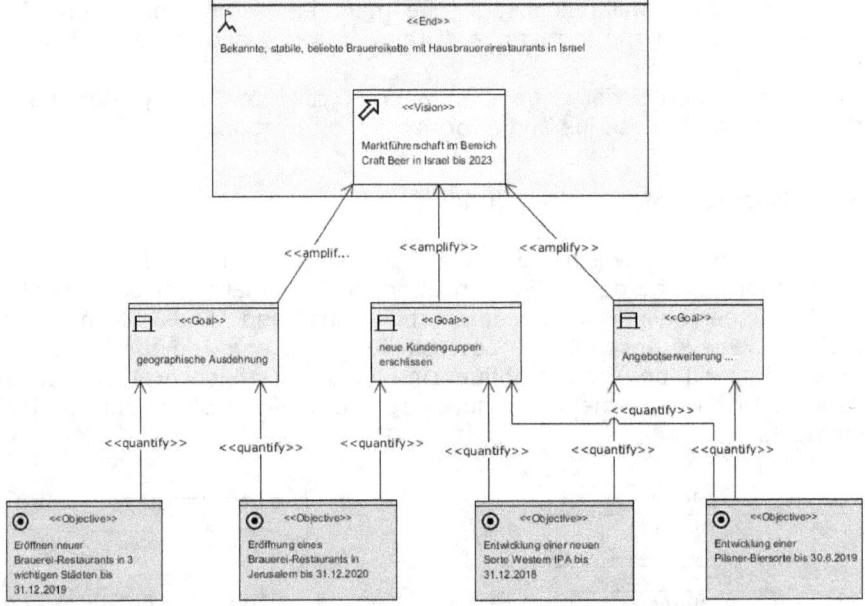

Figure 18: Motivation of FatBuddha described using BMM (Visual Paradigm)

Archimate® also contains elements for describing motivation and its interrelationships. Figure 18: Motivational Elements from TOGAF® (detail) shows a few elements of this class in Archimate®.

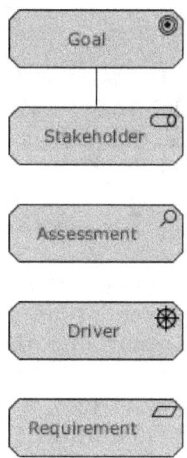

Figure 19: Motivational Elements in Archimate®

OMG standards (unfortunately) do not define any methodology. The BMM standard is a big exception. In addition to the elements, BMM provides guidance on the application of the standard - see Figure 20: Logical Progression through BMM. Behind this is a classic SWOT analysis- (**S**trengths, **W**eaknesses, **O**pportunities, **T**hreads). For more information consult the standard (BMM 2010) or (J. Pitschke, Unternehmensmodellierung für die Praxis: Band 1: Eine Einführung in die Darstellung von Unternehmensmodellen 2011). This also applies to the use of informal presentations. We have to evaluate and weigh up vision, tactics, goals, and objectives.

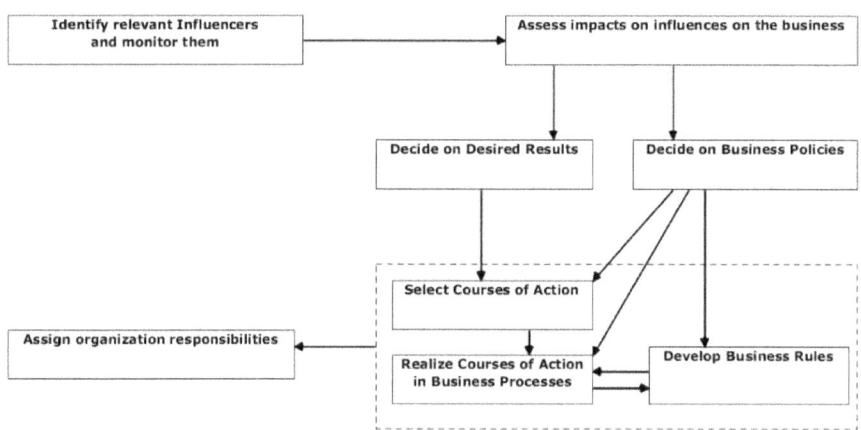

Figure 20: Logical Progression through BMM

What do I like about BMM? BMM speaks first of "influencers", not of the traditional stakeholders. "Influencers" are evaluated and monitored. "Influencers" can be rated positive or negative related to our project. Strengths or weaknesses, opportunities, and threats.

43

Sometimes the same "influencer" is both positive and negative evaluated.

Imagine, for example, that FatBuddha wants to grow organically. Employees are first selected internally for new positions. That's positive at first sight. Employees see the possibilities of career development within the company. The structure of the team keeps stable for a longer period. At the same time, this may be a negative factor (thread). If we want to expand the business, we may not find enough employees for the expansion.

If one influencing factor is "positive" and "negative" at the same time, it is particularly important that we prioritize based on the objectives and goals. What is more important to us? Organic growth or the possibility of faster expansion.

If we do not use BMM, I recommend this principle too. With customers, I often experience that the stakeholders are rated either positive or negative. Beware of this black and white thinking.

Assessment of goals and objectives is also essential to evaluate and weigh various, potentially conflicting goals and objectives, key performance indicators, risks, and other outcomes.

We need to know not only about the motivation for the organization. As a second cross-project model, but we also need to know the company vocabulary as the foundation for all the models we will build later. Whether business process models, value stream models, system requirements, or other models. In the mentioned style guide, we define naming conventions to name model elements and models. Building a Vocabulary (SBVR 2008) explains the basic concepts. Valuable tips and advice to develop and use a vocabulary can be in (Ross 2009).

4 Introduction to SBVR – The Vocabulary

The role of language in the development of models has already been emphasized.

Visual models are created from natural language and need to be translated back into natural language.

The vocabulary, therefore, plays a crucial role, both for the creation and the interpretation of the models. As the name of the standard expresses, the standard talks about two things: business vocabulary and business rules. If you look at the standard, the much larger part is devoted to vocabulary. Essential elements and concepts are briefly presented.

The standard SBVR follows the "mantra of business rules": "Rules are based on facts. Facts build on concepts. Concepts are represented by concepts." This may not be 100% correct, but it sketched the basics quite good.

4.1 Concepts and Terms, Synonym, Communities

First, we look at concepts and terms. A term represents a concept.

If we look at our example company FatBuddha, we have to understand the terms used. We do not want to become a professional brewer, but we need to develop a basic understanding of terms used in a brewery. What do we mean by brew, malt, punch, and other terms used?

Especially many problems are caused by concepts that everyone thinks to understand. An example is the term "customer". What is a "customer"? Are we talking about a legal or natural person? Is a prospect already a customer?

What is a term? A term is a word or phrase used in everyday communication in our organization to represent the concept. To avoid misunderstandings in communication, the term (better the concept) must have a clear definition, a clear meaning.

The term represents the concept. This concept is described by the term definition. The term represents the concept in normal communication.

In everyday communication, we use multiple terms for the same concept. We then speak of synonyms. A synonym is a word or phrase that can be used instead the original term in all contexts.

Sometimes we see the opposite question. We use the same term (the same word) to mean different terms. This is called a "homonym".

In practice, there are three problems in creating a vocabulary:
- It is difficult to find good and precise definitions free of ambiguity.
- The use of synonyms must be limited to simplify communication.
- When using homonyms, the context must be clear or stated to avoid misunderstandings.

The definition of a concept (a term) is not easy. This shows e.g. the definition of the terms "IT service" and "IT service provider" in the ITIL standard (see: (Foundation of IT Service Mgmt. Based on ITIL(R) V3 2007)) and www.itsmf.de).

"IT Service: A service provided to one or more customers by an IT service provider. An IT service is based on the use of information technology and supports the customer's business processes. ... "

"IT service provider: A service provider that provides IT services to internal customers or external customers."

The definition of the terms is circular, the definitions refer to each other. A good definition has the form "An X is a U, that ...". We present the definition in the form: "term: definition". The definition should not repeat the term to be defined. Whenever possible, we use generally accepted dictionaries and standards for the definition. This can be the Duden, the Brockhaus, (in English) the Merriam-Webster or subject-specific dictionaries.

Synonyms are unavoidable in practice. We try to keep the number of synonyms low. We name a term as a preferred synonym. Synonyms that we do not want to use in our models, we mark as forbidden or not desired. In practice, instead of "Incident" we also find the term "failure" or the term "trouble ticket". We define "Incident" as a preferred term, "Trouble Ticket" as a permitted synonym and "Failure" forbidden term.

Finally, the concept of "community" is introduced. A community is a group of people who use (or understand) the same vocabulary in daily communication. SBVR differentiates between natural language communities (German, English, Russian, etc.) and professional communities (the community Logistics, the community of Brewery). A specialized community can be an entire industry (for example, Logistics or Brewery), but also a single company or part of a company (for example, FatBuddha accounting). Communities should not be too small. Mostly the vocabulary applies to the entire company. Otherwise, communication within the company is difficult.

4.2   Facts and Fact Types

Many projects use a glossary that includes the terms used and their definitions. Depending on the tools used, the glossary is part of the models or exist in the form of a word list.

In a glossary, usually, the nouns (noun concepts) are defined. However, modeling projects show that we also need to define the relationships between the concepts and thus the verbs (verb concepts).

SBVR defines next to the terms fact types (Fact Types) and Facts. A fact type defines relationships between set objects. A fact type is named by a fact type symbol.

For example:
Bottle <u>is contained</u> in box
Customer <u>complains</u> about delivery
Customer <u>owns</u> maintenance contract

For the modeling of business processes and the definition of business rules, it is also necessary to describe relationships between individual concepts. For example.

The fact type "Country uses currency" is detailed by the facts "Germany <u>uses</u> Euro", "Switzerland <u>uses</u> Swiss Francs" ....

You need to know also the facts, to realize a rule as "The currency of the invoice must be the currency used by the country of the customer.".

There can be multiple fact types between two concepts. If several relations (facts) exist, they must all be presented and described.

4.3 Presentation of a Vocabulary

How do we represent a vocabulary? The SBVR standard deliberately leaves this open because the standard "only" defines the concepts of a vocabulary and business rules. The representation is explicitly not part of the standard, in the appendix of the standard different representation possibilities are shown. One is the Class diagram of UML. Modeling tools offer various forms and functions for definition and use of the vocabulary.

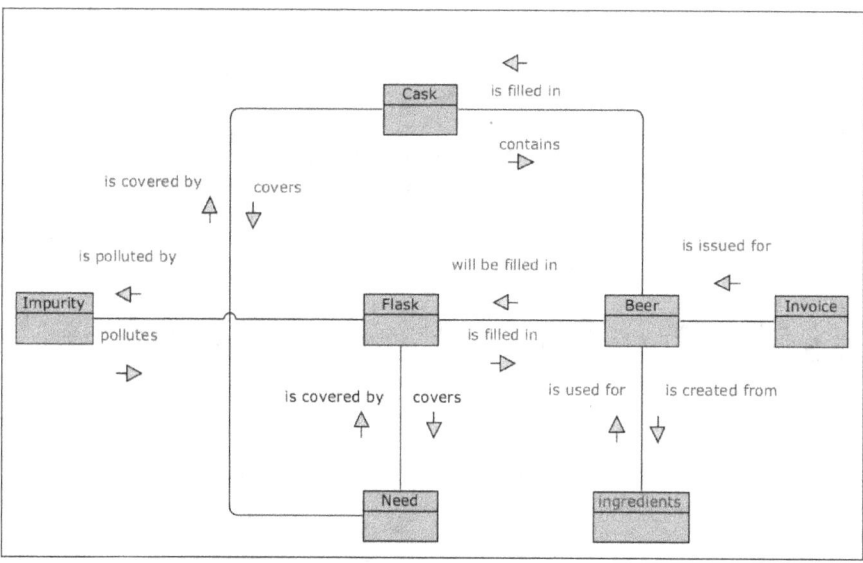

Figure 21: Fact Model (Example, Visual Paradigm)

47

4.4 Finding Terms and Facts for a Vocabulary

Having an idea of the description of a vocabulary now, the question arises, how do we find the elements the concepts and the relationships (the Facts) between them? How to construct the vocabulary? There are one (or two) helpful exercises for that:
- Ask your workshop participants to name the 5 most important terms for the area considered in the project.
- Encourage workshop participants to emphasize the most important term (the main concept).

As a result, we get five terms as the basis for our vocabulary. At the same time, we force the workshop participant to copy the project. What is really important?

From the definition of the terms we find new terms to be defined. In determining the most important terms, the strategy, the goals and objectives, and the project charter are essential (see 3.1, 3.2 und 6.1).

Once we have identified the terms, the question arises about existing relations (facts) of interest for our project. There may be several relations between the same terms. To describe the business rules and business activities in the business process gives us input fort he needed facts and vice versa. For example, there is a business rule "A customer invoice must be reported in the currency of the country of the customer's main office.". To understand the business rule and apply it correctly we need to know and understand different terms. What do we mean by a "customer"? What do we mean by a currency? What is the customer's main office? At the same time, we identify the facts, that is, the relationships between the concepts.

In order to identify these relationships, we look for connections described in existing texts. An example is the given business rule. In addition, we ask for different types of relations, e.g. the relations classification or part-whole relationship. (See also textual analysis in 6.8 Model Policy (Example)).

Type of Relation	Explanation	Example
Classification		
Specialization	a set of objects defined by the concept is decomposed into subsets	The Concept "Driver" is broken down into the subsets "car driver", "motorcycle driver", "truck driver"
Instantiation	a set of objects defined by the concept is instantiated by the enumeration of the instances. This is a possible and typical way	The concept "currency" is described in more detail by listing the possible instances "Euro", "USD", "SFr"
Part-Whole-Relation	An object defined by the concept contains	a "car" contains "engine"

		other objects (Terms)	
Association		there is a relation between two concepts most general relation in a fact model the relation must be named and defined	between the concepts "shipment" and "destination" the relation "is determined for" exist

Table 4: Types of Relationships in Fact Models

We are iterative in the development of our models. We only started with five terms. The vocabulary (terms and facts) grow over time. Regularly review the definition of terms and facts. The expectation that the first definition and collection of facts is complete and correct is hardly fulfilled. Make sure that the defined terms and facts are needed in our models.

5 Describing Business Processes

Having defied the basics (motivation, vocabulary) for describing the business processes used in the organization, we can start to present and describe the business processes. The most important standards for this are BPMN (for the presentation of structured processes) and CMMN (for the presentation of unstructured processes). First, however, we need to develop an understanding of what we jointly understand by a business process and what information is needed for business process management. Good sources of inspiration are (Sharp und McDermott 2008) and (Tregear, Reimagining Management 2018). You will find in the bibliography other very inspiring books regarding the subject. Especially (Tregear, Reimagining Management 2018) I like it very much. The presentation using the OMG standards (BPMN, CMMN) plays a minor role in the mentioned books. The representation of the processes is an (important) means to an end. The definition of the PO (Process Optimization) and the PI Cycle (Process Improvement) in (Tregear, Reimagining Management 2018) are very worth considering for your own work.

5.1 What is a Business Process? Types of Business Processes, Presentation forms

In the literature, the terms "business process" and "workflow" are often used as synonyms. The term "business process" emphasizes more the business (implementation-independent) description, the term "workflow" more the technical implementation (for example, with the help of a workflow engine). Interestingly, the BPMN and CMMN standards do not provide a comprehensive definition of the concept "Business Process". It should be remembered that the main content of the standard notations is the visual representation of the concepts and the interchange formats. For the definition, the literature of the term "Business Process" is more abundant. BPMN simply states Business Process as "A set of business activities that represent the steps required to achieve a business objective. It includes the flow and use of information and resources."

In the classics of business process literature, e.g. (Hammer und Champy 1993), various definitions of the term business process can be found. A definition based on the classics and very useful for our purposes comes from (ABPMP 2009):

"A (business) process, in this context, is a defined set of activities or behaviors performed by humans or machines to achieve one or more goals. Processes are triggered by specific events and have one or more outcomes that may result in the termination of the process or a handoff to another process. Processes are composed of a collection of interrelated tasks or activities which solve a particular issue. In the context of business process management, a "business process" is defined as end-to-end work which delivers value to customers. The notion of end-to-end work is critical as it involves all functional boundaries."

All definitions have in common that the exact sequence of business activities plays only a minor role. The sequence is important for some purposes, not all. Other information is more important. Essential for me are the following points:

- Business processes consist of a **set** of business activities.
- A business process has a defined result that provides value to the process customer.
- Business actors execute the business activities.
- There is a logical connection between the business activities. They serve the same purpose (of the entire business process) but do not have to have a fixed order necessarily.
- For business activities, stakeholders use technical systems and other resources.
- Each activity has a defined input (information, material) and a defined output. An input or output consists of multiple values and objects.
- Events play an important role. They initiate, signal the termination and control business processes.
- Business processes are not limited to a single department. The organization chart of the organization plays a subordinate role. We talk about end-to-end processes across all departments and involved organizational units. The goal of the process is important, not the organizational chart of the company and individual responsibilities.
- Business processes (at least those of interested in modeling to us) are repeatable with different scenarios.

5.2 Describing Business Processes – BPMN

There are many books about BPMN, for example (Allweyer 2009) or my old book (J. Pitschke, Unternehmensmodellierung für die Praxis: Band 1: Eine Einführung in die Darstellung von Unternehmensmodellen 2011). BPMN is extensively discussed. I don't want to repeat this here. Figure 22: BPMN-Palette (selected elements) shows important elements of the BPMN.

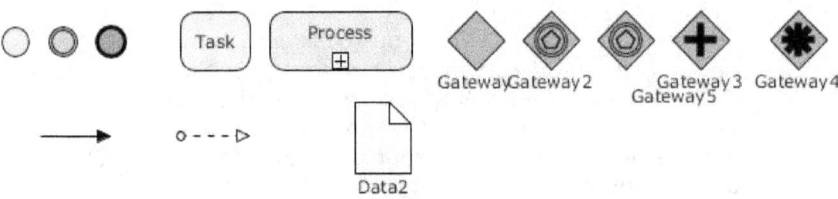

Figure 22: BPMN-Palette (selected elements)

BPMN emphasizes one aspect of the process description: the representation of business processes that have a fixed, predictable flow (with possible alternative and parallel scenarios). This is one important form of a business process in business operations, but not the only one.

Every company has such predictable standard processes. These are well suited for standardization. For such (standard) processes we can provide work instructions (Standard Operating Procedures (SOP)) for the employee. New employees easy to train. Other characteristics, such as the description of responsibilities, can be well described.

The routine is also a danger.

The description of the logical flow leaves questions open and requires the description of further attributes outside of BPMN. We also need to describe characteristics that are not related to the process activities but are important to our stakeholders. This may include information about risk, data protection, information about times and resources needed. The definition of so-called tagged values can describe such properties without leaving the standard. Textual descriptions, tables or color legends are used too. Just think of so-called heat maps or RACI charts. See 5.5.2: RACI-Charts– Responsibilities in the Business Process

We must (always) assume that our employees are intelligent. Therefore, we can ask how extensive, how detailed do we have to describe our business processes and single activities. Depending on the purpose of our models, we answer the question differently. Descriptions of security-relevant processes must certainly be more extensive. Again, be careful. Less is more: Business process models are often described in too much detail. For example, for one customer, I saw the activity "turn on machine" in the process model. Is that relevant? Depending on the purpose, this can be important.

In many cases, we describe processes too detailed. The models are therefore difficult to maintain (keyword "agility"), the effort for creation and maintenance grows, the acceptance among the users decreases. No user wants to be patronized and fight through confusing (because too detailed) models.

Scott Ambler coined in a discussion on LinkedIn the term "undermodel". Does your company accept (at least temporarily and depending on the purpose of the model) incomplete models? Beware of too detailed descriptions too early. This happens frequently and "by itself".

For a detailed description of the elements of the BPMN, I point again to my old book or to (Allweyer 2009). Our poster "BPMN for Business Analysts" (BCS - Dr. Juergen Pitschke 2006) is a popular source too.

Not every process can be precisely predicted and described in every situation. This applies especially to flexible, knowledge-intensive business processes. Then BPMN models become confusing.

5.3 Describing Business Processes – CMMN

Table 5: Structure of Business Processes; BPMN versus CMMN gives an overview of the difference between BPMN and CMMN. Every company has processes of both types. Completely unstructured processes are, in my opinion, the exception. If you ask a firefighter about my example "Chemical Fire" from the table, you will learn that, of course, there is an order. First, lives must be saved; after this, assets are protected. In doing the activities, we react to the current situation. Which type of fire is it (A combination of the Chemical Fire with Electric Fire?, People involved with danger for life)? The example belongs more to the category "Unstructured with predefined fragments". This category will for sure contain more examples which are more interesting too.

Structuring Business Processes			
Structured	Structured with Ad-Hoc-Exceptions	Unstructured with predefined Fragments	Unstructured
e.g. Customer Acquisition, Invoicing	e.g. Backoffice in Financial Services	e.g. Claim Settlement Sea freight, Bankruptcy	e.g. Chemical fire (Fire Brigade)
Predictable Repeatable	←——————————————————→		Variable Unique
Structured Data	Data / Documents / Unstructured Data		Unstructured Data
Control	←——————————————————→		Support
BPMN	BPMN	BPMN / CMMN	(CMMN)

Table 5: Structure of Business Processes; BPMN versus CMMN[2]

---

[2] (Kemsley 2012)

To get closer to CMMN, we need to understand the basic principle of modeling described in Table 6: Design Time versus Runtime (see also Table 5: Structure of Business Processes; BPMN versus CMMN).

Design Time	Single Scenarios and Cases (unstructured)
	Abstract, Formal Models
Run-Time	Specific, generalized Scenarios and cases
	Model Instances

Table 6: Design Time versus Runtime

First, we collect information about our processes, the participants, the objects used, etc. This can be done through various techniques (brainstorming, facilitation, interviews, questionnaires, observation, etc.). Next, we formalize this information and construct formal models out of it. In the case of unstructured, knowledge-intensive processes and the use of BPMN, the formalization is possible but time-consuming. The resulting models are complicated. It is hard to maintain. With the help of CMMN, the modeling of such business processes is easier; the models are easier to maintain. We do not describe (as in BPMN) a lot of fixed steps to describe the business process flow, instead we build a plan of how to organize the process flow when certain situations occur (which activities have to be performed in which order?). Such situations can also occur multiple times in the same process. For example, in describing a patient's medical treatment, it may happen that the patient loses consciousness. This situation can occur multiple times for this patient and the same treatment.

The elements are designed to describe such a plan. In the standard specification, this is emphasized. "In a particular situation to achieve a desired outcome. ... Planning at run-time is a fundamental characteristic of case management." (CMMN 1.1 December 2016). Figure 1: CMMN palette shows some CMMN elements. The current version of the standard is 1.1 (released 2016). Compared to version 1.0 (published 2014) the volume of the specification increased from 96 pages to 144 pages, unfortunately.

In addition to the (better) presentation of flexible, knowledge-intensive processes with CMMN, our stakeholders need to understand and accept the case models. This requires new, unfamiliar thinking about business processes. For some industries, the mindset of CMMN is more familiar. CMMN offers advantages for all industries.

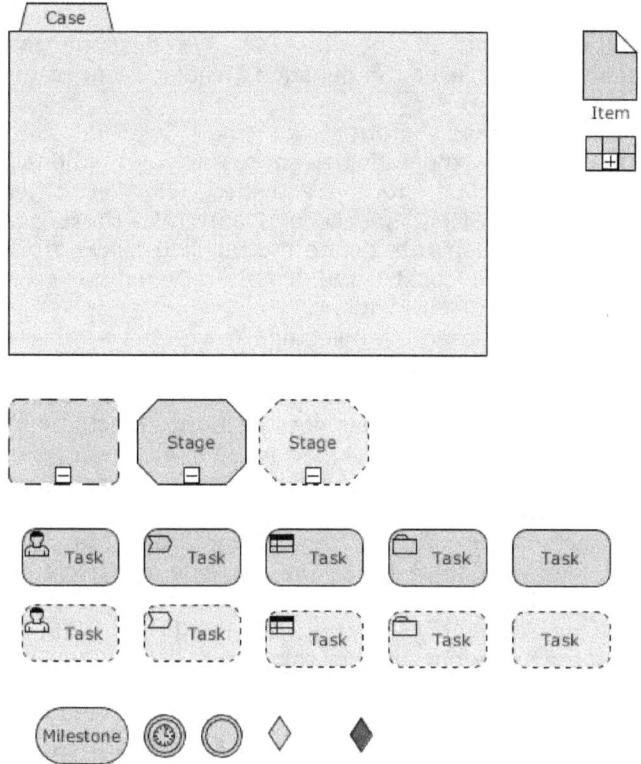

Figure 23: CMMN Palette

The most important elements:
The case element. The standard states "A Case is a proceeding that involves actions taken in a subject in a particular situation to achieve a desired outcome."

Note the similarity with our business process definition and the emphasis on situational awareness. The CaseElement (the Case) is the container that collects all elements for the case.

This includes the naming of the involved roles (actors, case workers) who are allowed to perform human tasks or who can trigger UserEvents. In the case "treatment of a patient" these are for example the roles doctor, nurse, patient, for the case "sea freight import" these are among other things the roles account manager, route planner, container operator, shipment operator. We know now the "Who?" for our case. Our approach is iterative. The first list of participants will not be the last.

The next important element is the CaseFile and the CaseFileItems, which are included in the CaseFile. A CaseFile contains all the information we need to plan the case and that describes the current situation.

CaseFileItems can be nested.

For example, a CaseFile for the "Patient Treatment" case contains the CaseFileItems Personal Data and Treatment Data. In the case of

55

"sea freight import" the CaseFileItems shipment record, Bill of Lading and customs clearance are part of the CaseFile. We describe the "what?". Our perspective is to answer the question "What do I need for the planning of the case?".

In addition to the case information (the CaseFile with CaseFileItems), we need to know the activities (necessary and optional) that make up the case. In addition to the activities, we need other elements to control the case. CMMN speaks of PlanItems. These are defined as "PlanItemDefinition elements define the building blocks from which Case (instance) plans are constructed. PlanItemDefinition is an abstract class that inherits from CMMNElement."

The first PlanItem is "Milestone". A milestone represents a goal to be achieved. It allows controlling progress in achieving the goal of our case and to control single activities. There is no direct work associated with a milestone. A milestone therefore does not represent an activity. A milestone is "guarded" by an entry sentry (see below). A milestone is typically characterized by a past participle that expresses the achieved state. In the example "Chemical Fire", the first milestone to be reached is "lives saved". All objects that represent living things are in the state "saved". Based on the achieved milestone, we can plan and execute further activities. The milestone can contain a large number of CaseFileItems in a defined state. It also serves to simplify modeling (a simplified description of the situation) and our thinking.

PlanFragments, Stages, Tasks represent activities (done work). EventListeners control activities in the case.

Stages and PlanFragmens are comparable to the subprocess in BPMN. They include multiple PlanItems. Stages are a specialization of PlanFragment. Unlike PlanFragment, a Stage can have a planning table (see below). A stage forms the context for planning. Plan fragments represent a pattern. For the moment we are particularly interested in Stages as a combination of several PlanItems.

Tasks are atomic ("A task is an atomic unit of work."). Tasks are divided into different types. Table 7: CMMN Task Types shows possible task types.

Task type	Explanation
Human Task	
Process Task	BPMN Compatibility; Process Tasks in a Case, described through a BPMN model; In the CMMN view this tasks are atomic;
Decision Task	DMN-Compatibility: describe the task through a Decision Service;
Case Task	CMMN-/BPMN-Compatibility Cases within a BPMN-Modell are described by this symbol;

Table 7: CMMN Task Types

A task has several attributes (properties).

Attribute	Explanation
isBlocking	If isBlocking = True, the Task doesn't have an Output
Inputs	
Outputs	
Performer	For HumanTask only

Table 8: Task Attributes

Be aware that some properties are not of interest for the business modeling. CMMN is also used for workflow engines (provided the workflow engine can interpret CMMN models (e.g., Camunda). As BPMN CMMN is used for both purposes.

It is interesting that for a task the attributes input and output are defined. Each BPMN task should have these attributes too. If we model (BPMN) processes or (CMMN) cases at a business level, each task must have an input and an output. At the implementation and execution level, this is not absolutely necessary.

In addition to the activities, events are of interest. The definition of Event is similar to BPMN: "... an event is something that happens during the course of the case. Events may trigger ... the enabling, activation, and termination of stages and tasks, or the achievement of milestones. Any event has a cause." Unlike BPMN, we do not distinguish start, intermediate, and end events. Intermediate and end events can represent an effect (an impact) in BPMN. In CMMN we represent this either through a milestone or through changes in the CaseFile (respectively the CasefileItems). A milestone is a summary of particular changes in the CaseFile. This describes a change in the situation. We distinguish again different event types:

Eventtypen	Explanation
Standard events	Changes/Transitions in the CaseFile or in a PlanItem
TimerEventListener	Time related Events; Definitions of points in time or Intervalls;
UserEventListener	Intervention of a User

Table 9: CMMN - Eventtypes

There are different possible transitions for the standard events (CaseFile: addChild, addReference, create, delete, removeChild, removeReference, replace, update, plan Item: close, complete, create, disable, enable, exit, fault, manualStart, occur, parentResume , parentSuspend, reactivate, reenable, resume, start, suspend, terminate).

To control a case, we need three additional pieces of information:

Some plan items (Stage, Tasks) have the property "discretionary" = true. Simply said, the execution is at the discretion of a CaseWorker.

Some PlanItems (Stage, Task, Listener, Milestone) are "monitored" by Sentries. A sentry is a combination of an event (on-part) and / or a condition (if-part). A Sentry can be an Entry Criterion or an Exit Criterion. In easy words: A sentry watches out if the situation changes and we have to react.

In the case of entry criteria (entryCriteriaRefs) the task / stage is activated, in case of a milestone the milestone is reached

For exit criteria (exitCriteriaRefs), the task / stage is terminated.

Planning cases is an important aspect of CMMN. Stages and tasks can have a Planning Table. The standard says "Planning is a run-time effort. A PlanningTable defines the scope of planning, in terms of identifying a subset of PlanItemDefinitions that can be considered as planning in a certain context. .. ". Planning Tables are described by DMN models. Planning Tables can be nested. They give guidance on which discretionary items to perform depending on the current situation. The standard defines only PlanItems as a result of PlanningTables. I can imagine that we need to decide on other aspects too. Which resource do we have to use? But this is not part of the current standard.

For a detailed description of CMMN refer to the standard (CMMN 1.1 December 2016) or our workshops (www.enterprise-design.eu; available as online course too).

The standard, like other OMG standards, gives no methodological hints. It doesn't define a method. After we have defined our basic business architecture and levels of detail, the question is, which business processes are processes well suited for BPMN-models, which business processes are "cases" and better described by CMMN. This question is at all levels of our detail (see 2.2 Detail Level).

How can we tell if we have a traditional business process (suitable for BPMN; for example, recording an order) or a case (more suitable for CMMN; e.g., bankruptcy of a borrower)? A rule of thumb for me is the first stakeholder interview. If we ask about the activities, talking with Stakeholders or Subject Matter Experts (SME) about BPMN very quickly and very detailed individual activities are described.

For cases (CMMN processes), when asked about the process, we often hear the answer "That depends ...". Then the SMEs describe what this depends on. They describe the framework for the CaseFile. They describe the possible situations that occur and the reaction to them. For example, in the bankruptcy example, the SMEs tell us that the activities and their order depend on the type of insolvency (bankruptcy, planned insolvency, bankruptcy with mass, bankruptcy without mass, ...).

Did we identify a business process as a CMMN process (as a case), we usually model "top-down". First, we determine which factors are relevant for planning the case. Which situations can occur? The focus in the first iteration is the CaseFile with the CaseFileItems. What is involved in the case? Then we identify the milestones we want to reach. The next step is to describe the activities needed to reach the next milestone. The order is unimportant to us at the moment. In the end, we reflect dependencies and the possible orders (flows; and flow conditions) and complete our CMMN model.

Remember: we work iteratively. The expectation that our first model is correct and complete is a fallacy, whether we develop BPMN models or CMMN or other models.

What can we learn for BPMN from this for? Even with BPMN models, it makes sense first to identify the milestones, then identify the necessary activities to transition from one milestone to the next. Then the order of activities is finally determined. BPMN does not provide an explicit element for milestones. In my workshops, I use Intermediate Events for this. These intermediate events are first of all a thinking and structuring aid. Whether we need these events in the final model is open. We will see.

I come back to a discussion about the acceptance of the models. CMMN is beneficial to many organizations and businesses. Everyone has unstructured, diverse, knowledge-intensive processes. Nevertheless, customers often use BPMN for this as well. The reason is the knowledge of the stakeholders. BPMN is already known through other models, through education and training, through guidelines. Stakeholders only want to deal with an additional notation when the benefits of CMMN are seen and realized. We need to demonstrate these benefits (greater flexibility, better maintainability), we need to support stakeholders with tools, such as legends that help to understand. The definition of examples and patterns that illustrate entire business processes or subprocesses are helpful too.

5.4 Operative Business Decisions and Business Rules

The importance of operational business decisions and business rules for the full description of business processes has already been stressed (see also 5.5.1: The IGOE concept). Both BPMN and CMMN connect to operational decisions, using DMN or other presentations of business logic. BPMN knows the task type Business Rule Task, CMMN knows the Decision Task Plan Item. BPMN, CMMN, and DMN are referred by the OMG "as the BPM trilogy". CMMN also uses DMN for describing the PlanningTables.

For the description of the business logic BPMN and CMMN are not suitable. Models that mix description of business processes and business logic are poorly maintainable. In architecture management of business architecture, we speak of the architectural principle "separation of concerns". For each content to be described, the appropriate form of presentation must be identified. (Barbara von Halle 2009) gives argumentation too why business process description and description of business logic needs to be separated.

5.4.1 Operative Business Decisions – DMN und TDM

For the description of operational decisions and the realization of the "separation of concerns" between business process description using BPMN and CMMN and business logic DMN and TDM are equally suitable. DMN is the standard notation by the OMG for describing operational decisions. TDM (The Decision Model) is a proprietary notation supported also by different tools (Qualiware, Bizzdesign). Figure 24: DMN Examples in Decisions First and SignavioFigure 3 shows a DMN example in DecisionsFirst and Signavio. Figure 4 shows a TDM example created in Qualiware.

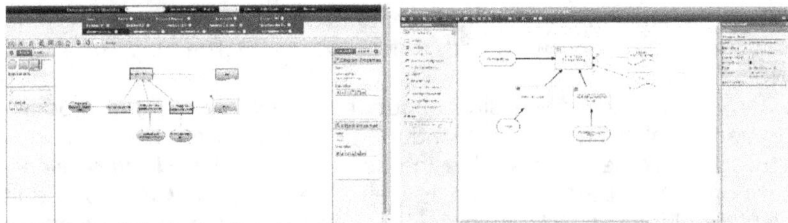

Figure 24: DMN Examples in Decisions First and Signavio

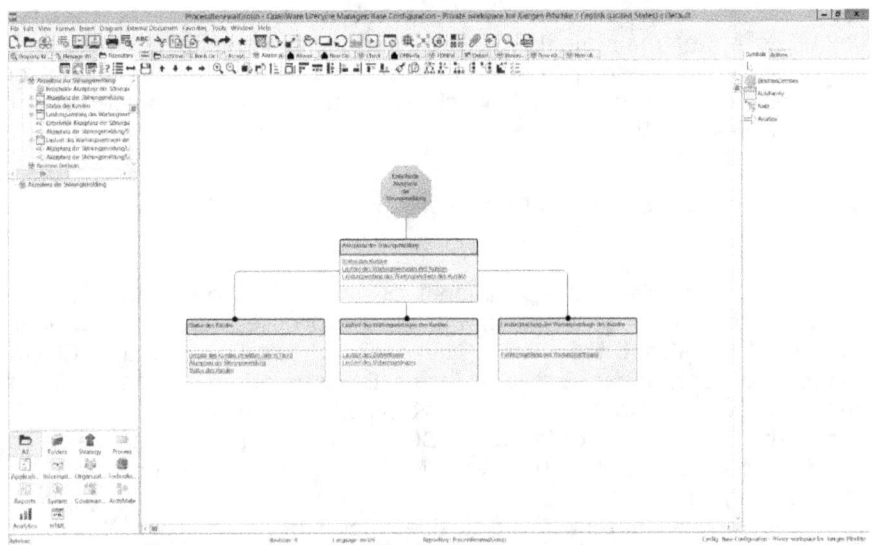

Figure 25: TDM Example (Qualiware)

Every decision has a question to answer and specifies the possible answers. The specification of the question and the possible answers is an important design step.

"Behind" the decision symbol in both notations a decision table is stored. The Decision Table describes the decision logic in form of a decision table. In TDM, a decision table is called RuleFamilyTable. We store additional information about the decision (other attributes needed to support the TDM methodology). DMN contains additional properties that provide more information about the decision table. For example, the number of results delivered by the decision table. If the table has multiple results, it specifies how to handle these results (average, determining the maximum, determining the minimum, other operations). Common to both notations is that decision tables contain the business logic is described in form os a decision table containing business rules. For the description of a decision table, there are different possibilities. Most modeling tools chose the horizontal representation form for representing business rules. Common to both types of notation is the fact that all rules in the decision table contribute to the same decision. This means the rules can have a different structure (different attributes). The only criteria is that they all contribute to the same decision.

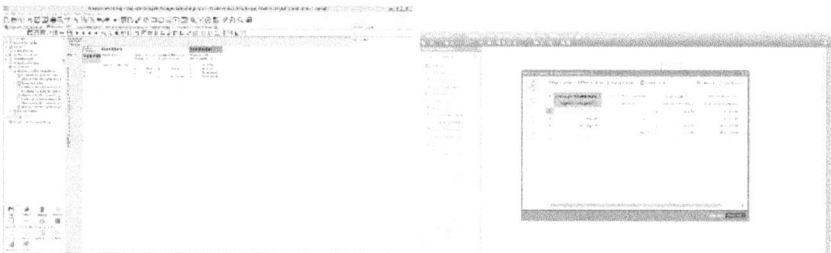

Figure 26: RuleFamily Table in TDM (Qualiware), Decision Table in DMN (Signavio)

The DMN standard can be found under (DMN 1.2 2019). DMN is supported by many tools (e.g., DecionsFirst, Qualiware, Signavio). A very good description of the elements and the application offers (James Taylor 2016). TDM is the acronym for "The Decision Model". TDM is a proprietary notation, but it is supported by several tools (Qualiware, BizzDesign) too. Notation and basic principles are described in (Barbara von Halle 2009). TDM has symbols other than DMN. TDM, however, is named "DMN compliant".

In the book, Barbara von Halle and Larry Goldberg describe "normal forms" and "basic principles" for the design of business logic using decision tables called RuleFamily. The correctness of the models and the decision tables is therefore already ensured in the design. DMN tools offer test functions to ensure correctness. Correctness is often "tested" "into" the models. However, nothing prevents us from applying the principles of Barbara von Halle and Larry Goldberg, even using the DMN standard notation. DMN provides some elements in addition to the TDM elements (for example, the Knowledge Source). A first description of TDM was already included in (J. Pitschke, Unternehmensmodellierung für die Praxis: Band 1: Eine Einführung in die Darstellung von Unternehmensmodellen 2011).

5.4.2 DMN Palette

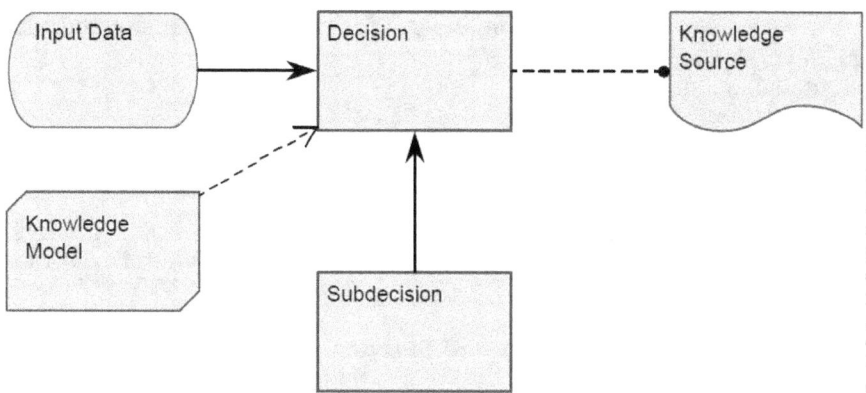

Figure 27: DMN Palette: Model Elements and Relations

Figure 1Figure 27: "DMN Palette: Model Elements and Relations" shows the model elements and relations of DMN. Not visible in the model are the attributes and decision related to the decisions.

It is noteworthy that the elements already contain the properties needed for the method.

5.4.3 DMN-Element Decision

First, we identify the decisions of interest us. These can be contained in the business process (compare the activity types Business Rule Task in BPMN and Decision Task in CMMN). Business processes can be simplified and made flexible if the decisions they contain are described explicitly and independently of the process. Decisions are also used outside of business processes. A Decision is characterized to describe a selection. The Decision is characterized by a question and a set of possible answers. Example are:
- Do we accept this error message?
- What price do we offer for this item?
- Who has to approve this application?
- Up to what amount can the loan be approved?

All these decisions are characterized by the fact that they are frequently done. This pays off the effort for managing and optimizing the decisions.

Another case of applications are strategic decisions, for example "Should we buy this company". The target of DMN is mainly decisions of the first group of examples - operational decisions. Optimizing and managing these decisions is important. The automation and digitalization of operative decisions are a frequent goal of use. Not every decision of interest is automated.

The other type of decisions - strategic decisions - is addressed primarily through decision support systems. It is important to provide information for decision-making (for example through dashboards) and to make the decision informed.

After naming the question, we specify the possible answers. There are several possible types:
- Individual values
- A range of values

When users begin to think of this question, they often think of yes-no answers. But Yes-No-Decisions are the exception. Answers should be as specific as possible.

In describing the question to be decided and the possible answers, the complex decision logic is not (yet) of interest to us. We follow a top-down approach.

5.4.4 DMN-Elements Input and Sub decisions

After we the specified question and possible answers, we ask what information we need. To answer the question two types of information may be necessary:
- Information that is directly available or available to us. For example, data or data stored in a database, which we simply (and also manually) learn about. To answer the question of whether a vehicle complies with the TÜV regulations, we consider, for example, whether there are rusted spots on the exhaust. This happens through "inspection" of the vehicle. For the description we use the DMN element "Input".
- Decisions sometimes require information that results from other decisions (from sub-decisions). The decision model describes a hierarchical network. We are going top down again.

We are still interested in the specific business logic only in so far as we ask for the necessary inputs, but not about the specific business rules: which values result in which decision result.

5.4.5 DMN-Element Knowledge Model

The specific business rules leading to a specific result (the business logic) are specified in a decision table associated with the decision. This decision table is not specified as a Knowledge Model. In addition to decision tables, other metaphors are used to describe the business logic. Examples are optimization algorithms or decision trees.

The Knowledge Model element allows the use of such metaphors and is therefore an extension mechanism of the DMN.

5.4.6 DMN-Element Knowledge Source

The Knowledge Source element tells us why our business logic (the decision table or other metaphor) was in the specific way designed by us. Knowledge sources can be legal requirements or policies. But knowledge sources can also be human sources such as "John", which serve as a source of business logic.

All in all, we follow a top-down approach, from the decision to be specified, definition of the question and the set of possible answers, through the input, the necessary sub-decisions to the specific business logic.

For the methodology and further information on the individual elements, see (James Taylor 2016)) and the Decision Management Manifesto (Taylor 2014)

5.4.7 Additional information for business decisions

We need further information beyond the DMN standard notation or the TDM notation. Similar to the RACI concept, we want to name responsibilities. For decisions, the "OMI" concept has been adopted. OMI stands here as an acronym for "O"wn, "M"ake, "I"mpacted by. Own refers to the organizational unit that specifies how the decision is made. "Make" refers to organizational units that make operational decisions in day-to-day business. "Impacted by" refers to organizational units that are influenced by the decision.

Other interesting information are:
- Frequency of decision: How often is the decision made? Operational decisions are made very often. However, the frequency and volume are very important to prioritize and decide if we are looking for automation for the decision.
- Change Frequency: How often does the decision change?
- The question of frequency, we also need for the risk assessment.
- Speed, Latency: Imagine accepting a customer's complaint. How long do you have time to decide what the best action would be to respond to the complaint? In such situations, it is not important to make the best possible decision. The decision must be acceptable and in line with our objective. Above all, it has to be made within a given time.
- Effort for testing and assessment: Some decisions can only be judged after a long time. Imagine the granting of a loan. Depending on the type of loan, the term is up to 30 years. Only after 30 years we know if our decision to lend was "good" or "bad". Building on the outcome of historical decisions is one way. Simulations are also a frequently chosen way for such scenarios - Do we change the decision criteria? How easily can we simulate results? Do the results meet our expectations?
- Complexity: The more criteria are included in the decision, the greater the effort required for description, testing, simulation, evaluation of the decision.
- Variability: How fast and often do the decision and the context change?

The application DecisionsFirst is remarkable with regard to such additional information.

5.4.8 TDM methodology

Barbara von Halle and Larry Goldberg define in the book (Barbara von Halle 2009) "normal forms" and "principles" of representation and analysis of decision tables comparable to the normal forms of relational database tables. The normal forms and principles ensure the maintainable, redundancy-free and consistent creation of such decision tables.

- First normal form (atomicity):
  Principles 1 to 4 are realized. A RuleFamilyTable cannot be decomposed into more than one line without losing content.
- Second Normal Form (Full Functional Dependency): Principles 5-6c. Functional dependencies exist only for the entire Rule Family.
- Third normal form (no transitive dependencies):
  No transitive dependencies

In addition to the normal forms, Goldberg and von Halle define principles for the design of a decision-making (Rule Family) Table.

5.4.9 Describing business rules in natural language

In addition to the representation in DMN and TDM rules are still described textually. (Pitschke und Ross, RuleSpeak® Guidelines-Grundlagen, Version 1.2 2009) and (Pitschke und Ross, RuleSpeak Satzformen, Business Rules in natürlich sprachlichem Deutsch spezifizieren, Version 1.2 2009) provide the basics for describing business rules in German language. Language is very diverse. RuleSpeak is not defining a graphical notation and is less formal than DMN and TDM and not focused only on decisions. By following the rules of RuleSpeak, we are already formalizing the business rules when capturing the rules. The importance of (natural) language has already been emphasized. RuleSpeak unfolds its strength in the first analysis steps (see Ronald G. Ross 2015)). Even when translating the rules from DMN or TDM into natural language, RuleSpeak is used to give explanations for our decisions.

In addition to the description of the business rules, RuleSpeak also provides the connection to the vocabulary (see Introduction to SBVR – The Vocabulary).

5.5 Describing Business Processes – IGOE Concept, RACI-Charts, other descriptions

I already stressed the importance of standard notations. The (OMG) standard notations not only unify the presentation but also define exchange formats between tools that support the standard. However, the standard notations do not claim to be complete for every situation. The main goal is the definition of notations and exchange formats. When used, the modeler must be familiar with and familiar with the concepts used. The definition of the basics is often not very extensive. Literature and other standards are often more informative. See my discussion about the term "Business Process".

In addition to the properties named in the respective standard notation, we find further attributes not contained in the standard notation. Since the times of UML, every notation has an extension mechanism - the stereotypes. Stereotypes extent attributes and / or associated functions. Stereotypes are supported by most tools in the market.

5.5.1 The IGOE concept

The IGOE concept is such a case. IGOE is an acronym for I (nput), G (uidelines), O (utput), E (nabler). These four properties must be known for each activity. The activities were described from the implementation or execution perspective. If we stay at the business level, input and output must be named. Without naming the input, our model is incomplete. If it is difficult to name the output, we have identified a potential for improvement. With input and output, we do not just mean a single value. An input can include many individual values. Discussing CMMN I already mentioned that a business activity must name an input and an output. Depending on the used tool we need to check which extension mechanism is offered, cause BPMN isn't taking this into consideration.

The next missing letter in the acronym is "G". Naming the guidelines
for the activity. The meaning of guideline depends on the current level of detail. If we model at the management level (see 2.2 Detail Level) Guidelines are "Policies". Policies are not actionable. They define the context of the activity and the business rules. If we move on to the Operator level, Guidelines are more specific, they are actionable, defining business rules or operational business decisions. I will devote myself later to the topic of business rules and operational decisions. When describing activities at any level, the focus of "Guidelines" is to give guidance on how to perform the business activity. When describing activities at any level, the focus of "Guidelines" is to provide guidance on how to perform the activity to comply with compliance and legal requirements. In any case, it is about guidance and not patronizing the process executives.

The last missing letter "E" in the acronym stands for Enabler. Enabler are objects and resources that we need to run the process. In my brewery example, we need a forklift to load the beer boxes (with the beer bottles or pallets) onto trucks. When we look at the simulation of business processes, we think a lot about this aspect. There are different types of enabler. Sometimes they must be available else the process cannot be performed. Sometimes they have an impact on the quality of the process. Sometimes enabler are human resources, machines, information or other resources. Enablers are not changed by the process and are available again when the process is complete. Enablers may be required to run the process or have an impact on the quality, duration, and other properties of the process. Besides the simulation, the naming and evaluation of the necessary enablers is important for the improvement of business processes. Suggestions can be found for example in (Sharp und McDermott 2008). Sharp and McDermott name the following classifications of enablers:

- Workflow design
- Information Systems
- Motivation and Measurement
- Human resources.
- Policies and Rules
- Facilities Design

Depending on the situation and the company, other classes of Enabler are conceivable (Situational Awareness and Enterprise Awareness; (Ambler and Lines, Disciplined Agile Delivery: A Practitioner's Guide to Agile Software Delivery in the Enterprise 2012)).

Workflow Design is the core message of the process model, whether we use BPMN, EPC, swim lane diagrams or like forms.

I would take that further today: systems of information management and telecommunication systems. Today we talk about the digitization of business processes. We mean not only the automation of business processes but the development of new possibilities and the redesign of business processes using technical solutions.

Motivation and Measurement: I already emphasized the importance of motivation (3.1: Motivational Elements). Just as important is the measurement of the business process result. This does not just mean the needed time.

Human resources include knowledge, experience and development opportunities of employees.

Policies and Business Rules: Describing business rules and business decisions, are at Sharp and McDermott enablers. Because of their importance, IGOE considers them as own item.

Facilities: Not only the possibilities of technical systems have a big influence on the outcome of the business process. The organization of workplaces is of great importance.

Compare the ideas of IGOE in (IDEF0 1993) (a very old standard) and (Burlton 2001). The IGOE concept is supported e.g. by the tool Qualiware.

5.5.2 RACI-Charts– Responsibilities in the Business Process

Another typical question by customers is the question of responsibilities in the business process. Often a RACI chart is used for this. RACI is an acronym for "R"esponsible, "A"ccountable, "C"onsulted, "I"nformed. Wikipedia further specifies concepts based on it, for example

RACI-VS, which include other responsibilities ("V" stands for Verify, "S" for sign-off). Since this is not a fixed standard, everyone is free to name other responsibilities depending on the purpose of the model. Many tools include the ability to create RACI charts.

5.5.3 Business Processes and Risk Assessment

Do we describe business processes, risk considerations are important. The way of assessing risk is very dependent on our project assignment (see 6.1: Project Charter).

A risk is an event that endangers the business, its capabilities and business processes. Such an event is characterized by a probability of occurrence.

Doing a risk analysis, we follow these steps.
1. Risk Identification
2. Risk Analysis
3. Risk Planning
4. Risk Monitoring

Part of business process modeling is the identification of risks. In (Burlton 2001) the following classification is proposed:

Risk Type	Explanation
Commercial	Loss of market share or market advantages.
Strategic	The strategic plan of the organization is compromised.
Financial	Financial losses occur or financial benefits cannot be realized.
Technical	Used technical platforms are endangered.
Legal	The organization is exposed to legal regulations and is subject to investigation.
Political	The organization violates governmental regulations. The Political Surroundings change.
Fraud	Fraud threatens the organization.
To Image	The public image of the organization is compromised.
To Capability	The organization is unable to maintain or acquire the required human resources.
To Scalability	The organization is unable to increase or maintain market share.

Table 10: Risk Types

Risks can be classified to several types. Other types or subtypes may be relevant depending on the project charter.

Once we have identified the relevant risk types and detailed on a project base, we assess the likelihood of the risk occurring and plan our response to occurrences of the risk.

If risk through appropriate measures can be completely eliminated, we optimize our business processes and capabilities (see Section 6.9.2: Governance - Business Process Optimization and Business Process Improvement
). Often, risks cannot be completely avoided. It is also an option to delegate a risk. Depending on the risk, we select a service provider who takes over the risky part of the business process. The service provider should be better acquainted with the type of risk we face. By improving our processes, we can and want to reduce the probability of the occurrence of the risk.

At the same time, we plan the reaction to the occurrence of the risk. This can be the definition of additional business processes or the implementation of new technical systems. Here is an example of two-way links (see Section 6.3: Links between Models). Business processes are the source of risks. Other business processes define the response to the occurrence of the risk.

5.5.4 Customer Journey Maps

Another popular tool currently are "Customer Journey Maps". These models describe the experience of the customer (emotionally). The business process is divided into phases (stages). The process has several "touchpoints". Touchpoints are interaction points where we assess the response of one or more people to the impact of our business process. We assess the process from an (external) person. The other notations presented (BPMN, CMMN, DMN, etc.) describe the business processes primarily from the internal perspective (How do we organize our work internally?), while in "Customer Journey Maps" we describe the impact of business processes on external stakeholders.

Customer Journey Maps" are not a formal standard notation, although the realizations in different tools are very similar.

The origins of customer journey mapping go back to marketing. The number, name, and meaning of the phases are not fixed. Typically, the "awareness" phases (we make the user acquainted with our product and services), "favorability" (we make the customer more interested), "consideration" (the customer want to buy), "intent to purchase", "conversion" are differentiated.

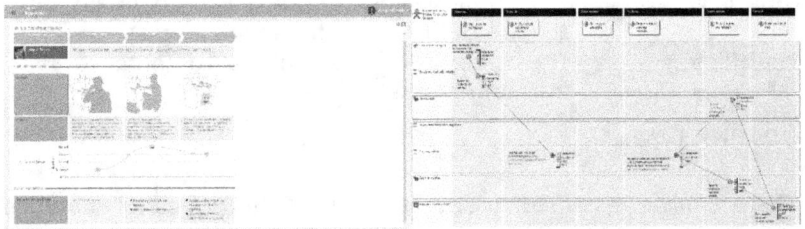

Figure 28: Customer Journey Maps (Examples; Visual Paradigm, Qualiware)[3]

5.5.5 Other descriptions

Much other information is gathered in the tools depending on the purpose of the models. In addition to information on the cost of the business process (price, duration), this can be information on the General Data Protection Regulation (GDPR) and the details of the necessary activities. Risk assessments and information for ISO certification are often in demand. Information about KPI and measurements of performance are included. Models are a necessary tool but cause a lot of effort. We have to justify the effort by the achieved benefits. For this, measuring and rating are mandatory. In a post in the Business Rule Community ((Tregear, Business Rule Journal. Vol.20, No.5 2019), Roger Tregear stresses the importance of measuring to make Process Optimization (PO-Circle) and Process Improvement (PI Circle) a success. "The most important question is "what's the problem we're trying to fix?" and we must have a detailed, specific answer. Compare (Tregear, Reimagining Management 2018). Thinking about meaningful measurement and rating can also help to reduce the cost of modeling. Is it necessary to describe each business process in detail on each level of detail and in each abstraction (see 2.2 Detail Level? If we are not convinced of the benefits of the details of the models at an abstraction and a level of detail, we do not describe these models or not yet in detail (under model). We have to be critical. Of course, it is not possible to describe and evaluate all processes at the same time. We prioritize the business processes to be modeled. Which business processes give the most significant advantage for improvement and optimization?

Scott Ambler isn't speaking primarily about business process management, but his statements are not just relevant for the modeling and implementation of software systems (Ambler and Lines, Disciplined Agile Delivery: A Practitioner's Guide to Agile Software Delivery in the Enterprise 2012).

The additional descriptions (Priorities, Risk, ...) are not part of the BPMN or CMMN. These are proven forms of presentation (such as RACI) or proprietary descriptions. Here the tools differ considerably, depending on the area of application and the scope of support.

5.6 Describing Organization Structures

The Chandler-based quotation "structure follows process follows strategy" existing in different variants enjoys great popularity. The basic message is that the starting point of our considerations is the strategy

---

[3] Sources: https://www.visual-paradigm.com/solution/customer-experience/customer-journey-mapping/ and
https://coe.qualiware.com/templates/customerjourneymap/

(see 3.2: Business Motivation Model). Based on the strategy, we define processes. The structural design of our organization must not define the definition of business processes.

However, many business process management questions also require a description of the organizational structure to identify potential for improvement (see, for example 5.5.2: RACI-Charts– Responsibilities in the Business Process).

In the tools used in the book, it is possible to describe the structure of the organization through an organizational chart, to establish and evaluate links to other descriptions.

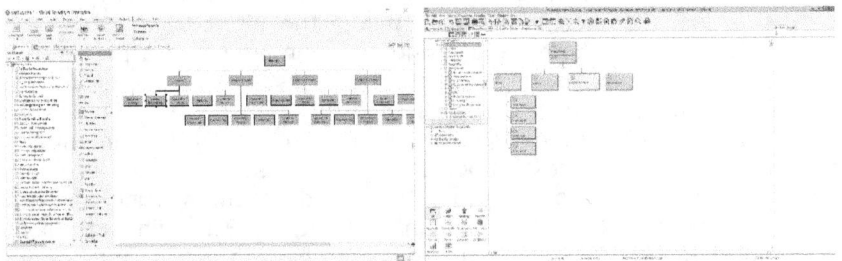

Figure 29: Presenting Organizational Charts in Visual Paradigm and Qualiware

5.7 Business Capabilities

In the previous chapters, I introduced a set of descriptors and standard notations that depict various content used to describe different views in business process management. A single view of the business process is not enough. Which additional means of description we need depends on our project.

In addition to the choice of suitable means of description, the question arises of the connections between the individual views and elements. For the selection of content and connections we use the Zachman framework (see Chapter 2: The Zachman Framework). The basic elements in the Zachman framework are so-called primitives (or atomic elements), as opposed to composite elements. Whether an element is atomic or a composite element also depends on the chosen level of detail (see Section 2.2: Detail Level). If we look at objects in the "how" abstraction in the structural view, we consider business processes as elementary objects. If we look at these processes in the operators view, the business process consists of various elements (activities, events, roles, resources, and others. The business process is therefore a composite object in this case. The link between the levels of detail is realized by decomposition and detailing. In Section 1.4, Figure 3: Burlton Hexagon to describe a Business Process Centric Capability, we have already come to know the Burlton Hexagon for describing Business Process Centric Capabilities. The statement is also that the description of a business process requires different views and artifacts: Policies & Rules, Intent and Strategy, Organizational Structure, Supporting

Infrastructure, Enabling Technology, Human Capital. In recent years, various organizations and companies have promoted the use of "capabilities" as an elemental (atomic) object. The details of the description of a capability are given at lower levels of detail. Accordingly, in the perspective of "business scope" and structure level, we speak and use "capability maps". I feel positive about it. It makes clear that the description of several views is necessary for professional business process management. Examples of such efforts include the BIZBOK ™ (Business Architecture Guild 2013) and the current glossary of the BIZBOK ™ (Business Architecture Guild 2019) and the efforts of the Open Group ((The Open Group 2016), https://publications.opengroup.org / p161). In the Glossary of the BIZBOK™, "capability" is defined as "particular ability or capacity that a business may possess or achieve a specific purpose or outcome." (after Ulrich Homan). The illustration in Figure 3: Burlton Hexagon to describe a Business Process Centric Capability describes in more detail which artefacts are associated with a business process. BIZBOK™ and (The Open Group 2016) differ in the detail of the necessary information. My experience is that every company has different rules set out in the style guide and the modeling guideline (sections 6.5 and 6.6). BIZBOK™ names Customers, Partners, Competitor; Vision, Strategies, Tactis; Capabilities; Policies, Rules, Regulations; Organization; Information; Initiatives, Projects; Value streams; Products. Services; Metrics, Measures; Decisions, Events. In (The Open Group 2016) the following picture is shown:

Figure 30: Competence-Capability-Resource Relations (Source (The Open Group 2016))

The capability concept is a continuation of the IGOE concept. In addition to the input and output, the guidelines and enablers, we need further elements of the context of the business processes. Both approaches include "soft" factors. Example is the culture of the organization. Or information associated with business process management as measuring the quality and performance of business processes.

5.8 Describe Business Processes - Business Process Pattern

In 5.2: Describing Business Processes – BPMN and in (J. Pitschke, Unternehmensmodellierung für die Praxis: Band 1: Eine Einführung in die Darstellung von Unternehmensmodellen 2011), we saw a brief introduction to BPMN. BPMN is generally considered a universal notation for describing business processes. The notation defines "only" the basic elements, unifies the presentation and defines an exchange format. (see (OMG 2016) and Figure 22: BPMN-Palette (selected elements).

BPMN describes "only" the fundamental element of a business process, unifies the presentation of these elements and the meaning and defines an exchange format. We also describe business processes at higher levels of detail (see 2.2 Detail Level). Models of the higher levels of detail consist of the basic elements. We describe related business processes. To simplify the modeling and standardization of the models, we define "patterns" that represent recurrent situations in the same way again and again. In BPMN we can do this with the help of subprocesses. Another possibility are so-called "patterns" or "templates".

"Pattern" repeats and combine different primitives, and another pattern (or template). They increase the readability of business process models.

An example of such a pattern is a "Follow-Up". A follow-up always shows the same procedure and the same process participants. What is different is the object to follow-up: Sometimes we follow-up on an invoice, sometimes on a customs declaration, sometimes on another "object". I already showed the "follow-up" as an example for a pattern on our BPMN poster (see (D. J. Pitschke 2012) and Figure 31: Business Process Pattern - Follow-Up). The figure shows the business process pattern).

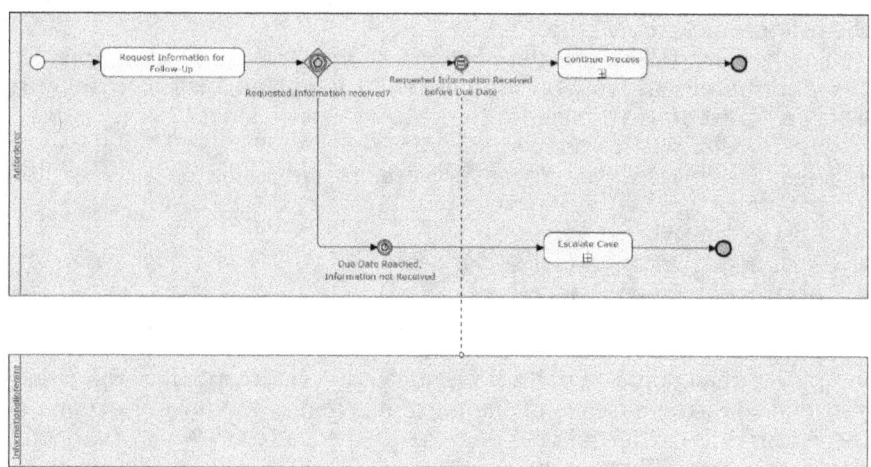

Figure 31: Business Process Pattern - Follow-Up

You can think of more such patterns. Darius Silingas of NoMagic has named more such patterns. An example is a "Competition Pattern".

A "competition" can happen, for example, when hiring a new employee. We write out a vacancy, fill in the required qualifications of the candidate. From the detailed applications, we do a preselection. From this preselection, we decide then for an applicant.

The same happens from the business process point of view when purchasing a device. Here the competition object differs. We are not looking for an employee but wish to purchase a device. The process is the same. It is a pattern. Based on defined, required properties, we receive a series of offers for the device (the device type) from which we first do a preselection. Finally, we decide based on specific properties for the device to be purchased.

5.8.1 Definition of a business process pattern

Various business process modeling tools provide functions for defining and using such patterns. First, we have to think about which patterns we want to offer, to make the effort worth and the advantage of using patterns is realized. I have already mentioned two examples here: follow-up and competition. What is similar in both cases? How can we describe such a pattern? How can we identify such patterns?

Uniform is the described flow of the business process. The elements for describing and controlling the process are the same. Depending on the pattern variants can be defined.

Variable is the main object of the pattern. In the case of the follow-up, the "object of the follow-up". We use the pattern "follow-up" for various concrete objects. For example, an invoice or a reminder or a customs declaration

The participants of the process are maybe variable too. As in the case of objects, we try to find a generic term. The respective role is later replaced by real process participants. For example, by the recipient of the bill or the customs officer.

Since we follow the classification of the Zachman Framework (2: The Zachman-Framework), the question of variables is easy to answer: which abstraction is variable for the pattern, which is not?

- Abstraction What: variable; see above
- Abstraction How: not variable, variants are admitted to a limited extent
- Abstraction Where: variable
- Abstraction Who: variable
- Abstraction When: variable
- Abstraction Why: can be variable; is usually not variable for a pattern

The definition of a pattern includes a brief description of the stable part and fives the essence of the pattern. What is the flow of actions of the pattern? What is the real purpose of the pattern? Which (variable) part causes a possible variant?

We name the variable parts of the pattern. Not every abstraction has to be variable for the pattern. We always try to find a generic term. Depending on the abstraction, the name of the pattern will help: For example, "Follow-Up object".

In summary, we can say that a business process pattern is characterized by the fact that the flow of actions is the unifying feature. The name of the pattern clarifies this. What is the same for all "Follow-Ups"? What causes variability or specialization? Example: "Follow-Up on invoice". Forming such subsets and classifications helps identify part patterns or variants. In our style guide we define which patterns we use and what is the real content.

5.8.2 Business Process Pattern in Visual Paradigm

Visual Paradigm allows the definition and use of model patterns, named there as templates.

To create such a template, we select the elements of the business process model that belong to the pattern. From the context menu we choose "Define Design Pattern".

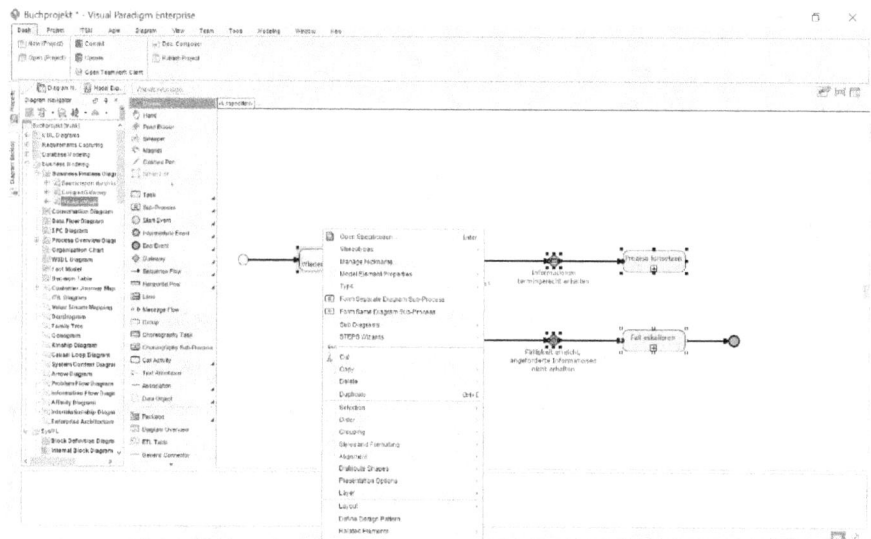

Figure 32: Defining a business process template in Visual Paradigm

When defining the patterns, we can (and should) provide a description. For this we can use description templates in the usual form. We select where the pattern should be stored - in the workspace or in a directory. It is recommended to create a directory for all templates (a template library) that is accessible to all project members.

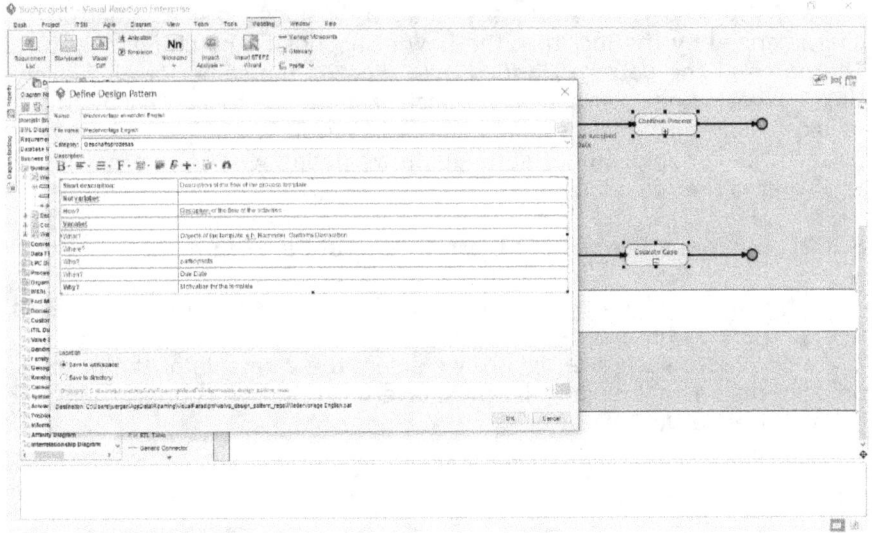

Figure 33: Describing a template

To apply the pattern, select Utilities-> Apply Design Pattern from the context menu and select the pattern. The description of the pattern should help us here. The patterns are additionally categorized according to the notations used. All elements used in the template can get new names.

We can define patterns for all supported notations. In business process management, for example for CMMN or decision management. For development with UML, Model View Controller (MVC) is a common pattern. More detailed information on using templates in Visual Paradigm can be found in (Visual Paradigm, Inc. 2019).

5.8.3 Complex Business Process Patterns – Example: Return of an Online Article

The two business process patterns presented (follow-up, competition) are simple in nature. They include one notation (BPMN) only and focus on one level of detail. More interesting pattern containing several notations and abstractions. An example is the "Complaint of a Web Article". This combines several notations and abstractions as partial patterns. The overall pattern consists of the description of the business process described using the standard notation CMMN. What activities are executed and in what order depends on the situation: First, we need to find out, if the item can be returned. Was the ordered item already shipped, packaged or not? Did we receive the item back? Do we need to evaluate if the item can be resold or if repairs / renewals are necessary? Within the business process described with CMMN are several business decisions needed, described using DMN.

The definition of the pattern is the following: First, describe the business process model represented by a CMMN diagram. We specify the required information as part of the case file model. We define milestones for structuring the case.

Next step: we specify the business decisions included in the business process and use DMN diagrams. Finally, we specify the details of the necessary activities and the conditions. The overall pattern then consists of several sub-patterns: one for the CMMN diagram and one or more for the DMN diagrams.

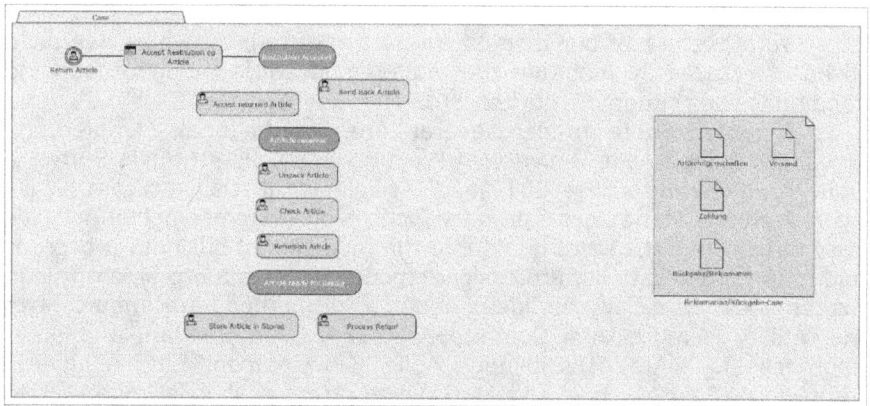

Figure 34: Brainstorming for CMMN-Pattern Return of an Article

Figure 34: Brainstorming for CMMN-Pattern Return of an Article shows the result of the first brainstorming for such a pattern.

Such a procedure is also recommended for business process modeling using BPMN. First we identify the necessary activities without defining the order of the activities, we describe the order of activities and necessary conditions and the details of the activities later. I stress again that modeling is an iterative approach. Good models arise through repeated questioning and improvement.

6 Methodology and Agility

Enough of the descriptions. If we look at different tools, we find many other notations, informal or standardized (see chapter 7: Tools). Under the catchword "Agility" maintenance and creation of models in a flexible way is addressed.

To make use of our models and to profit from the value, we need to be able to easily maintain the models and adopt them to changing conditions (See (Roger T. Burlton 2017)).

I quoted Scott Ambler several times in the book (Ambler and Lines, Disciplined Agile Delivery: A Practitioner's Guide to Agile Software Delivery in the Enterprise 2012)and DisciplinedAgileDelivery.com. While Scott Amblers/ Mark Lines's primary focus is on systems engineering, it's easy to translate the statements into the modeling of business processes and entire organizations. Professional modeling plays a prominent role in Scott's book. Especially his ideas about agile methods are important to me. Agility is more than Scrum, SAFE, LEAN, XP, Kanban, and other approaches). DAD "Disciplined Agile Development" is a hybrid framework. Scott Ambler and Mark Lines stress that it is important to choose the "right" approach. Because DAD builds on a variety of best practices, the user must be "Enterprise Aware" to select the methodology that best suits his needs. He can choose from several methods ("Choice is good."). Furthermore, the topic of architecture is essential. In DAD there exists a role "Architecture Owner". If we organize a modeling project, we also have to own and fill this role.

6.1 Project Charter

Project charters are presented and described in various forms. If we do not know about our goal (our mission) and which goals and objectives are more relevant (have a higher priority than another), we build on sand.

In TOGAF® ("Preliminary Phase") the "Statement of Work" is important and heavily discussed. The Statement of Work does not just describe what we want to accomplish (Architecture Vision). The Statement of Architecture Work defines the scope and measure we use. The Statement of Architecture Work serves as the basis for a contractual agreement between the supplier and consumer of architecture services. The Statement of Work includes the "Architecture Principles". I named some principles earlier. "Separation of Concerns", "Using different Abstraction and Levelof Detail" are two of them.

Many methods start a project with the project charter and contains principles for creating the project. In PMBOK (Project Management Institute 5th Edition 2013) a project begins with the "Project Charter", in (Ronald G. Ross 2015) it is the "Policy Charter." You find many templates and patterns in the Internet for Project Charter described textually and enhanced with graphic elements. This is also done in Visual Paradigm. In chapter 3.1 Motivational Elements we saw

"Motivational Elements" who are the basis for formulating the project charter.

The Project Charter is also starting point for "project governance" (see 6.9: Governance – Approvals, Maintenance). The project charter determines not only the required content of our models, but also the measures and principles to ensure our models are in sync with reality.

6.2 Content, Presentations, Structure

In Chapter 2, "The Zachman Framework," I introduced the architecture framework I use. I've been stressing that other frameworks do the job too. We chose the Zachman framework in our projects and workshops because it is method-neutral (as opposed to TOGAF) and provides a good grid for determining the model content we need to fulfill project charter. In Table 3: Simple Models and Artifacts in the Zachman Framework" I named typical content. The table is not complete.

However, the first step in the project is the naming of the model contents, which we want to create depending on our project charter.

	What?	How?	Where?	Who?	When?	Why?
Scope						
Business Concepts						
System Logic						
Technology Physics						
Components Assemblies						

Table 11: Define needed Content

Often the representation of business processes is the starting point for our project and given by the management, even if the goal is the implementation of software solutions or other technical systems. Business processes define requirements for the implementation of technical systems, business processes are the basis for improvements and assessments. The importance of business processes has been extensively discussed in the literature. In the literature list, you will find many suggestions. Especially (Tregear, Reimagining Management 2018) and (Burlton 2001) should be mentioned again. In addition to the automation and support of business processes through software systems, there are many reasons to describe, improve, and evaluate business processes. The reasons range from certifications (ISO, ITIL, and many others), verification of conformity (GDPR, others), risk management to optimization and improvement.

In addition to the description of the processes in the strict sense (primary content), the process models are connected to the vocabulary. The process models use the concepts defined in the vocabulary. In order to understand the process models, we must create a vocabulary ("What?" Abstraction, see chapter 4: Introduction to SBVR – The Vocabulary.

Whether we need to fill the models for further columns (abstractions) and enrich the process models with more information depends on the purpose of the models and the project charter. Sometimes it is the stated goal for our project to define and describe processes independently of another abstraction. If, for example, we are responsible for the management of the branches of a wholesaler, we would like to describe the processes in the branches independently of the location of the store and to make them uniform. The "where?" Abstraction and the relations to the process model are not of importance for this project.

Is the content determined (Which abstractions do we need?), we decide on the notations. BPMN and CMMN are available for the description of business processes (see chapter 5). Instead of BPMN, companies use EPC (event-driven process chains) or proprietary representations. In addition, we need more information to fulfill the purpose of the project (secondary content).

Once the contents have been determined, we determine how the relations between the abstractions are organized. The tools offer different possibilities. Also, content that exists outside of the tool (files in various formats (PDF, PNG, ...), web content) provide valuable information and must be linked to the models and model elements. To determine the needed model content the "storytelling" technique described in the next section can contribute.

6.3 "Storytelling" - Collecting Information

Once we identified the information (information types) we need to fulfill our project charter, we need to gather information about processes, business objects, decisions, and other artifacts. I already named various options for this: interviews, observations, workshops, process mining, playful techniques or a combination of these and other techniques. Sometimes it helps us to start with a "wrong" or incomplete model (see 6.8: Model Policy (Example)). In most cases it is easier for the involved stakeholders to name and improve incomplete and flawed models and model elements.

"Storytelling" is a popular working technique. Described for example in (Martin Sykes 2012). Such a technique requires a relaxed atmosphere. If our project or workshop participants find it difficult to tell "stories", tools will help. In (Martin Sykes 2012), "Story Maps" are shown (also for download) on the Internet at the book page book www.martinjsykes.com/storiesthatmovemountains. In addition to the content per se (the Why, What, How, Where, Exceptions: What if), information on prioritization and planning is provided (Sense of Urgency, Delivery Plan).

Combined are the story maps with questioning techniques. The questions to be asked can also be found on the named website.

If our workshop participants still find it hard to find and tell stories, another tool offers support, the so-called "Rory's Story Cubes" (at amazon.de too).

Figure 35: Rory's Story Cubes (Samples)

Participants roll dice with 3 or 4 dice and then tell a "story" that contains the diced pictures. The cubes are available for different topics. The topic does not really matter. It is important to stimulate the imagination and to start the conversation. For this, cubes not related to the topic are sometimes more helpful than related ones. The formalization of the information in models takes place in a later step. The questions named on the story maps support the later formalization.

6.4 Relations in the Architecture

For the connection between models and model elements, we differentiate between different types of relationships:

6.4.1 Refinement

Refinement is a relationship between a model-element and a model. The basic principle of refinement is that we describe the model element in more detail through another model. We stay in the same concept. In BPMN we know the model element Sub-Process, which we describe again by a process model (same concept). It should be noted that we remain in the same concept (here business process management). This does not mean that we necessarily use the same notation for refinement.

6.4.2 Adding Details

Adding Details again is a relationship between a model-element and a model. In contrast to "refinement" we change concept and notation to describe the element in more detail through other models.

An example is UML and the Unified Process. There, we describe Use Cases more detailed by, for example, adding sequence or activity diagrams that illustrate the Use Case more precisely (but with a different view). We change both the concept used and the notation.

6.4.3 Logical Relations

In addition to refinement and adding details, we want to realize and evaluate logical relations. This can be both element-to-element relations and element-to-model relationships. An example is the question which activity in the business process is linked to which system function.

6.4.4 Relationships in Tools

Tools support the principles mentioned (Visual Paradigm: Subdiagram, Reference, Transit; Qualiware: Associate; NoMagic: Hyperlinks, Inner Elements). Refinement and detailing use in most cases the same technical function. The difference is that we stay in the same concept with a refinement. With adding details, we change the concept (artifact). A Style Guide defines which relations we model and evaluate in our business architecture.

6.5 Structure - Classifications

When defining business processes and business process patterns, we need to structure the respective processes. Classifications of activities help us with this task.

In our workshops, I always emphasize the importance of good structure. "Structure, structure, structure, ..." is more important than the perfect mastery of the respective notation. The prerequisite for a good structure is to use a good classification. We already learned about different classifications. We distinguish between processes that are well predictable and those that are not? (Cases). At the highest level of detail (see 2.2: Detail Level) in the process map, we have applied a classification that we can also apply to individual activities (core process, management process, support process. In doing so, we differentiate business processes according to the type of process (core process, support process, management process). Especially at low levels of detail, we need more classifications to support structuring. Such classifications are used alternatively or together.

A classification of activities that has proven in projects and workshops can be found in (Debra Paul 2006). Activities are classified according to their primary task type. Classes are
- Planning Activities

- Enabling Activities
- Doing Activities
- Monitor Activities
- Controlling activities

This classification helps us to specify a meaningful order of activities at the lower levels of detail. First, we are looking for the "Planning Activities". For brewing beer, for example, this involves planning the ingredients that we need for each type of beer. For a Bock beer or a Christmas beer, we may need different ingredients or a different way of preparing the raw materials. Once we have planned our process instance, we determine the "Enabling Activities". What activities must be completed first in order to start the business process. In the case of our brewery, this includes, for example, providing the empties (bottles, casks) in sufficient quantities to bottle the beer. Only in the next step we determine the "Doing Activities": Which steps are necessary to brew a beer? In the "Monitoring Activities" we monitor the other activities; both the "Doing Activities" (e.g. Is the temperature when brewing as planned?) as well as the "Planning Activities" and "Enabling Activities" (e.g. "Are the empties cleaned according to the hygiene regulations? Do we have enough empties?). The "Controlling Activities" control the other activities. They are especially relevant if we see a gap in the process parameters. In addition, this classification can be combined with other classifications. Similar to the classification of Paul / Yates, the following classification is proposed in (Ould 2005):

- Planning Activities
- Reporting Activities
- Monitoring Activities
- Scheduling Activities
- Resourcing Activities
- Prioritizing Activities
- Negotiating Activities
- Reconciling Activities

The classifications can be mapped to each other. Both give help in determining the necessary activities. (Ould 2005) is a bit finer. Interesting to me is the class "Reporting Activities". Often users are thinking too late about reporting activities. In particular, for compliance with legal requirements, the implementation of these activities is important. Is the necessary information available for the reports and analysis? (Ould 2005) not only defines this classification, but also identifies roles of process participants who are responsible for the particular class of activities. As roles he names:

- Boards
- Managers
- Management Teams
- Management Teams
- Supervisors
- Progress Chacers
- Planning Teams
- Programme Support Offices

- Monitoring Groups

In addition to the classification of activities, we receive another classification that helps us to design the RACI charts, to name and identify the roles of process participants.

These classifications are no dogma, but a good guide.

Classifications are popular with users. They are familiar to us. They appear to us in many forms. They are the basis for structuring business processes and other artifacts (for example, operational business decisions).

In addition to the general classifications mentioned here, we find many classifications that are content dependent on our project order. For example, if our project assignment is the description of the business process from the point of view of the General Data Protection Regulation (GDPR), we classify the individual activities according to whether they are relevant to data protection or not.

6.6 Architecture Principles, Style Guide, Model Policies, Model Governance

I already mentioned some essential architectural principles in the book. Some (important to me) are summarized here. See also (The Open Group 2011).

Architecture Principle	Explanation
Separation of Concerns	Different concepts are described separately. One example is the separation of BPMN / CMMN process models and the description of business logic models with DMN or TDM. Models with different release cycles are separated and organized in multiple models.
Refinement **Adding Details** **Logical Relationships / Reference**	Refinement, adding details, logical relationships support the principles of "separation of concerns" and "structuring / limiting the scope" of models. The refinement and "Adding Details" are used within a perspective only (since this establishes a parent-child relationship). In case of relationships between perspectives, "Logical Relationships" or "References" are

	used.
Structuring	The repository is structured. Models are represented on different levels of detail. The naming of the levels of detail expresses the intended purpose. All project members follow the defined structure. Classifications are used intensively. Classifications are base for structuring all types of artifacts.
Structuring/Limitation of size	The size of each model is limited. The number of elements depends on the selected notation, abstraction and level of detail.
Common Vocabulary / Definitions	A Common Vocabulary defining the terms used in the models is defined. The vocabulary is used for a consistent naming convention too. The vocabulary is defined and used across projects.
Use of Colors	Color tags for identifying attributes (e.g., priorities) are used sparingly. Legends explain the meaning of such colors.
Reuse / "Single Source of Truth"	Model elements and models are reused. Redundant descriptions of model elements must be avoided.
Collaboration	Models are created collaboratively and shared across the enterprise. Models are created together and shared with stakeholders. Stakeholders can comment on the models but not edit them actively
Stakeholder orientation	Models serve stakeholder needs. The content of the models must be rich enough to fulfill the tasks of the stakeholder. Proven means of representation are preferred. Outputs are designed in form, structure, and content according to the needs of the stakeholders. The Stakeholders specify content and form.

Structuring / Classifications	Structuring and Classifications are important in all phases of the modeling process; Structuring and classifications are defined for the repository as well as for the content;

Table 12: Architecture Principles

The architectural principles define the general rules for organizing the business architecture (the models, and model elements used, the used relationships between models and model elements) of the enterprise. In (The Open Group 2011) it is emphasized that not too many architectural principles should be defined ((The Open Group 2011), chapter 23.6). These principles frame the policies of the company and are implemented and made practical in the style guide and the modeling guidelines. These principles are detailed in the style guide and the modeling guidelines to make them applicable (manageable). Following the (The Open Group 2011), architectural principles include a "rationale" (not contained in Table 10: Architecture Principles).

To assist our modeler developers, to ensure model consistency and maintainability, we provide three tools:
- A style guide (Which notation and notation elements do we use?)
- A modeling policy (How do we develop models? Which techniques do we apply?)
- Model Governance Rules (How do we structure and maintain the models?)

All three documents build on the architecture principles and help with their practical and uniform implementation. The documents give help and guidance to create compatibility and maintainability in the team.

The style guide regulates, how we use notations and model elements. We define patterns and templates. We restrict standard notations. The style guide describes simple things too. E.g., the use of colors.

The modeling policy gives help on how we do things. It explains working techniques and soft skills and their use.

The governance rules ensure the conformity and maintainability of the models. Many rules and "ceremonies" play a role.

All three documents require an understanding of the roles of project members involved and are built on the architecture principles.

The following section gives a suggestion and example of a style guide. Style guides are diverse, customer-, tool- and notation specific. The example in this book is general, using mainly BPMN. Are you looking for suggestions for a UML-style guide, I suggest (Ambler, The Elements of UML 2.0 Style 2005).

6.7 Style Guide (Example)

...

Organization of the repository:

The repository is organized in two levels by the element Model. The "Model" elements is a stereotyped package containing models (diagrams) and model elements. The "Models" define a physical structure of the repository. All modelers have to use the defined structure. An additional logical structuring for different purposes can be defined (Visual Paradigm: Logical View, Bookmarks; NoMagic: Smart Package; Qualiware: Folders)

At the top level, we follow the perspectives of the Zachman framework, in the second level, we structure for the domains (the content of the models). For example, logistics, gastronomy, brew-to-delivery,... We add models (containers) for the following artifacts:

Model	Explanation
Reports and Analysis	This model structure includes all models and outputs used for reports and analysis. These include RACI charts, report templates, generated reports.
Working Area	This model structure contains models that serve to test ideas, working techniques, or temporary content. These models are to be transferred to the content structure after checking (copy) or deleted after completion. Models that have been in this area for more than three months without a note will be deleted by the administrator.
General (Enterprise-wide) Vocabulary	The vocabulary must be used for the naming and description of the model elements. The vocabulary is cross-project (enterprise-wide) and becomes imported as a linked project. To keep the vocabulary manageable, it is structured on the second level for "domains" (areas). For structuring the element "Model" is used again. Each term used has a definition. The use of synonyms must to be limited (maximum of 3 synonyms per term permitted).

Table 13: Structure of the repository (Example, Style guide)

All modelers must use the defined repository structure. If the modeler misses a Model (Container) in the structure, it is necessary to coordinate the definition of new Models in the project team (governance, responsible role: Architecture Owner).

Figure 36: Repository-Structure (Example, incomplete) shows a possible structure of the repository applying these principles.

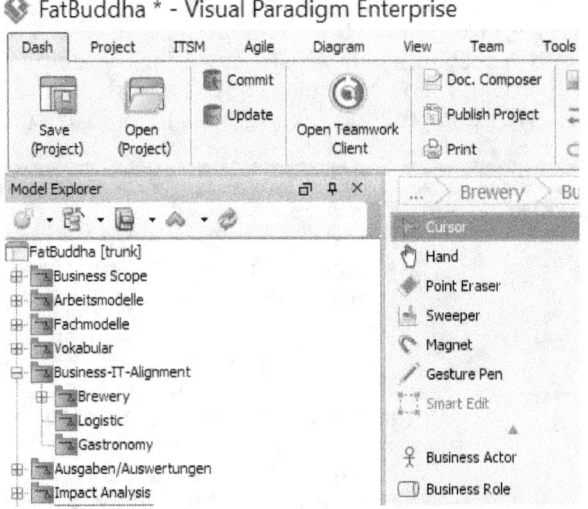

Figure 36: Repository-Structure (Example, incomplete)

If the model elements and models to be linked are organized within the same perspective (the same "Model"), "Refinement" or "Adding a Detail" is applied. When linking elements between perspectives, we use the function "Reference" in Visual Paradigm to add details and other views.

Figure 37: Use of References and Refinement

...
BPMN is used only at the management level and the Operative Level. Generally, we follow the specification of the BPMN (BPMN 2.0 2010) and the recommendations of Allweyer (Allweyer 2009) for the use of BPMN elements. We use elements which belong to

the analyst conformance level (see (BPMN 2.0 2010)). The elements are further restricted.
The number of elements (capabilities, value streams, sub-processes, tasks) per model is limited. The view of the Scope perspective are "Capabilities."
Capabilities are named by nouns. Examples are "handling empties", or "financial management". In visual Paradigm so called "Process Maps" are used.
A Capability is subdivided into a maximum of 10 value streams at the structural level. Each Value Stream at the Structural Level is decomposed into to a maximum of 15 activities in the Management-Level. The majority of the Management Level activities are Sub-Processes. The sub-processes of the management level are decomposed into a maximum of 15 tasks. A further decomposition does not take place. The activities of the operational level are tasks only. If the numbers of used elements are exceeded, the structure must be reviewed.
The complex gateway is not allowed at any level of detail. A corresponding configuration file is provided for the tool Visual Paradigm, which removes the elements from the general element palette.
[The ban of the "Complex Gateway" is caused by the fact, that it often leads to misunderstandings. (Serge Schiltz 2017) shows an example for using the element Complex Gateway:

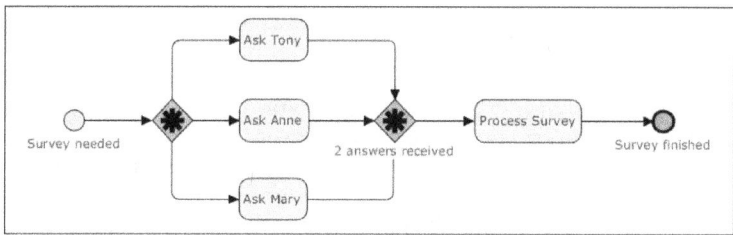

Figure 38: Use of a Complex Gateway (Example, Visual Paradigm)

What happens if you receive the third answer later? Do you execute "Process Survey" again? You need to answer this question. Your stakeholders (the recipients of the model) have to understand and interpret the model in the same way. To avoid ambiguity, we don't use the complex gateway.]
...
Each BPMN model must have a closed sequence flow per pool from the start event (the start events) to the end event(s). Each model must have at least one start event and an end event. Multiple start and end events are allowed.
...
Pools are named with the name of a process participant (for example, "FatBuddha", "Logistics") or by a general process role. Examples are "buyer" or "supplier".

Lanes are used only at the operative level. Lanes describe roles for the business process and are in no way to be mixed with departments (department names) or rea persons. Valid names include brewer, customer contact, logistician. Invalid labels are department names such as "Export" or "Marketing" or persons as "Mr.Miller". Lanes are linked via Transitor (Visual Paradigm) to organizational units in the organizational chart connected.

...

Events: Events are denoted by a << noun >> << past participle >> combination. Valid names are "order received" or "complaint answered".

For events, the trigger of the event must be specified. Permitted triggers are Message, Timer, Error, Conditional.

Depending on the trigger, the type of event must also be specified (catching, throwing).

...

The name of an activity is intended to express the planned result. Examples are "clean bottle" or "bottle beer". The principle you often read in the literature is, a verb-noun-combination is used for naming an activity. This rule is correct in general (see my examples), but maybe incomplete in single cases. The names of a business activity must express the planned outcome and must follow the fact model (the vocabulary). In addition to the noun-verb combination, this maybe a noun combination with a verb. An example is "load shipment into container". The relations between the objects must be defined in the fact model (vocabulary).

...

The given examples are for illustration only and are an excerpt from a complete style guide. The primary purpose is to define how content is presented. Which naming conventions do we apply for model elements and models? Which elements of the chosen notation do we use? Which elements are forbidden? How are models and model elements related?

6.8 Model Policy (Example)

The model policy gives us assistance to do different steps on the way from collecting information to a formal model. An example of this is the "textual analysis" (BCS - Juergen Pitschke 2012) or the usage of business process patterns. There is a variety of techniques for both gathering information and formalizing into a model. Examples were already given.

...

Textual Analysis

We first collect information. This can be done through interviews, questionnaires, observation, workshops. In interviews and questionnaires, we ask specific questions. This must also apply to workshops. The analytical approach described in (Abbott, An Integrated Approach to Software Development 1986) first published in (Abbott, Program Design by Informal English Descriptions 1983) also serves us to formulate specific questions in workshops or questionnaires.

In his Article, Abbott writes:

„We identify the data types, objects, operators, and control structures by looking at the English words and phrases in the informal strategy.
1. A common noun in the informal strategy suggests a data type.
2. A proper noun or direct reference suggests an object
3. A verb, attribute, predicate, or descriptive expression suggests an operator.

The control structures are implied in a straightforward way by the English."

Part of Text	Model Component	Example
Proper Noun	Instance, Object	J. Smith, Euro
Common Noun	Class, Type, Role	toy, currency, seller
Doing Verb	Operation	buy
Being Verb	Classification	is an
Having Verb	Composition	has an
Stative Verb	Invariance-Condition	are owned
Modal Verb	Data Semantics, Pre Condition, Post Condition or Invariance Condition	must be
Adjective	Attribute Value or Class	unsuitable available
Adjective Phrase	Association, Operation	The customer with children, the customer who bought the kite
Transitive Verb	Operation	enter
Intransitive Verb	Exception or Event	depend

Table 14: Textual Analysis (Abott)

We can also use this technique for different standard notations. We consider which model element types we are looking for and how we recognize them by normal language.

Model Element	Phrase	Sample
Use Case Diagram		
Actor	Noun (active object)	The service engineer ... The user ...
Use Case	Noun – Verb	... report incident ...
Association	Context	The user reports an incident ...
Class Diagram / Object Diagram		

Class	Common Noun	Currency
Object	Proper Noun	Euro
Association	Adjective, Adverbial Phrase	... the service engineer responsible for the incident ...
Composition / Aggregation	Having Verb	... has a ... ... belongs to ...
Generalization	Being Verb	... is a ...

Table 15: Textual Analysis (UML elements)

Model Element	**Phrase**	**Sample**
Pool / Lane	Noun (active object)	... the development department... ... the service engineer ... ... the customs officer ...
Event	Time Phrase, Conditional Phrase, Intransitive Verb	At 2 a.m. ... when receiving the confirmation ... ... if the confirmation is not received within 24 hours...
Activity	Verb-Noun Phrase	... buy goods ... ... archive document ... ... submit customs declaration ...
Gateway	Conditional Phrase	If a resolution is known for the incident, ... If the order volume is bigger than 20 TEuro, ...
Data Object	Noun (passive object)	... the invoice ... ... the service level agreement ... ... goods ...

Table 16: Textual Analysis (BPMN elements)

The principle is continued for more notations. Whether standard notation or informal description.

The elements are first identified as a "candidate". Than, the candidates are evaluated for relevance before being used in model elements and models. A critical assessment ensures that we really need the identified model elements in our models.

The textual analysis technique is supported by different tools, such as Visual Paradigm.

In order to facilitate the finding of activities (sub-processes and tasks), the activities are assigned to different categories (Debra Paul 2006):

Category of Activities	Explanation
Planning Activities	Activities necessary for the planning of business processes; For FatBuddha, for example, this involves planning the types and quantities of seasonal beers.
Enabling Activities	Enabling Activities ensure that the necessary resources are available for the killings, including human resources; For FatBuddha, for example, this is the management of empties and the qualification of master brewers.
Doing Activities	The activities that directly belong to the business processes of the "business perspective", as we already explained, we form subcategories (management activities, core activities, supporting activities) according to the purpose of the business; FatBuddha involves the actual brewing of beer (Brew-to-Delivery) and closing contracts with restaurants (Contract-to-Pay)
Monitoring Activities	Activities for measuring process quality; FatBuddha measures the number of complaints or measuring the produced amount.
Control Activities	Activities necessary to react to deviations in the monitoring.

Table 17: Activity Categories (Source: (Debra Paul 2006))

Structuring / Classifications:
Structures / classifications are represented by tables (for simple classifications) or by a dendrogram (for multi-level or multi-dimensional classifications).
Numerous working techniques use classifications. If classifications are multilevel or support multiple views, dendrograms are preferable.

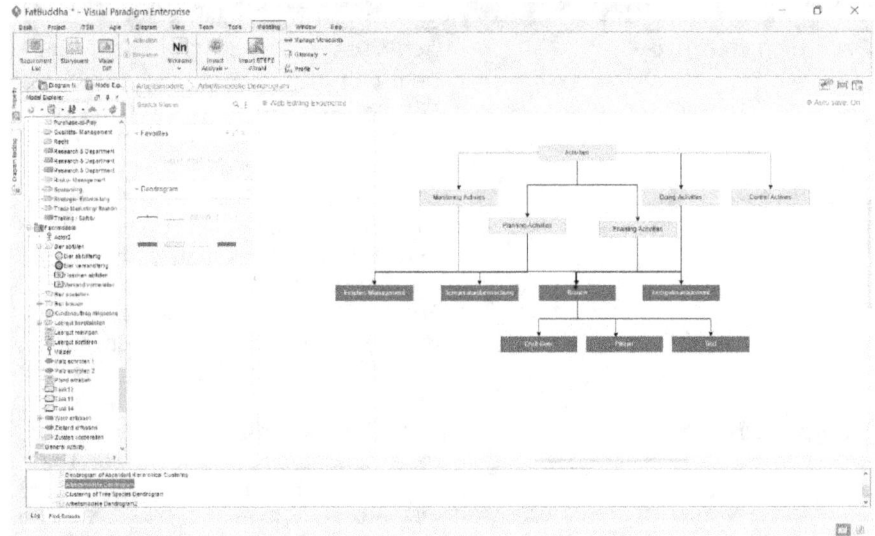

Figure 39: Multi-dimensional Dendrogram (Visual Paradigm, Sample, in progress)

6.9 Governance – Approvals, Maintenance

Another essential question is summarized under "Governance". The term "governance" is vague. It summarizes all steering and control mechanisms that ensure actuality of the models and their compliance with regulations of the company (Guidelines, Modeling Policies). This includes many "ceremonies" and rules (four eye principle, approvals, version management, daily stand-up meeting).

Such ceremonies involve planning, review, release and maintenance of models. We plan the release of models or parts of the models at defined times (milestones). We also define the expected quality criteria upfront.

In Figure 10: Quality criteria of models (selection), quality criteria for models have already been named. In addition to "hard" criteria (syntactic correctness, semantic correctness), "soft" criteria also play a role. For example, "fittedness" (does the model fulfill the intended purpose?), "Contentment" (does it only contain elements that we really need?), "Acceptance" (are the models accepted and understood by our stakeholders?). Our release mechanisms must take this into account. Will models be rated during the release after such "soft" criteria too?

In Figure 10: Quality Criteria for Model Assessment I named quality criteria for model quality. In addition to "hard" criteria (syntactic correctness, semantic correctness), "soft" criteria are relevant. For example, "Comprehensive" (Does the model fulfill the intended purpose?), "Contentment" (Does it only contain elements that we really need?), "Acceptance" (Are the models accepted and understood by our stakeholders?). Our release mechanisms must take this into account too.

In addition to the assessment of the quality of the models, we look at the process of creating the models in "Retrospectives". Which working techniques were successful? Which not?

Many (All?) modeling tools include project management capabilities too. If these functions are included in the modeling tool, a media break is avoided. For these tasks, however, other tools are often used, for example Jira®/Confluence. We have many similar questions to answer. E.g. the question "How do we structure and scope our project?". In the white paper "Using Confluence and Visual Paradigm" I show how we can manage the media break between the two tools. (D. J. Pitschke 2019)

Is a model released, the model must be "frozen" (Subsequent changes are prevented). Most modeling tools provide mechanisms known from default version management (e.g. creating a tag). If changes are made to the models (for example, to optimize business processes), work is done in a "branch". Only when the models are released and confirmed the models are synchronized into the "main branch". For this to be successful, releases and synchronization must be done frequently and regularly. Synchronizing the current models only after a long time can be difficult. Releases (partial releases) are therefore better in shorter cycles.

The release of models follows the usual principles of project management. Releases offer a good opportunity to involve stakeholders. An iterative procedure is suitable for modeling projects. I already stressed that the procedures described in "Disciplined Agile Delivery" (Ambler and Lines, Disciplined Agile Delivery: A Practitioner's Guide to Agile Software Delivery in the Enterprise 2012) are well suited. Although DAD focuses on software development, many principles are valid for business modeling projects too. In doing so, we always have to be "Enterprise Aware" and "Situational Aware" observing the current situation. In (Lines Mark 2018) Scott Ambler and Mark Line say: "While Scrum prescribes the use of a set of ceremonies," as the daily coordination meeting (scrum), iteration (sprint) planning sessions, retrospectives to be done on certain cadences within the iterations (sprints), Lean does not prescribe this overhead and instead suggests that it be done if and when necessary.".

Simple organizational rules can help in the governance of models. An example is a re-release of a model at least once a year. The cost of approvals must be less than the cost of creating the models.

We need mechanisms for team collaboration.

A review must follow strict rules. It must be prepared upfront. Which quality criteria are important for your project?

Finding errors should not be confused with overly criticizing models. If only criticism is given only the time required for a review increases. For sure you find good successful things in the project too. I refer to (Bono 1999). Such simple mechanisms as the "Six Thinking Hats" help to organize model reviews and avoid the mentioned problem.

6.9.1 Governance – Processes and Models

In (John Jeston 2008) an entire appendix is dedicated to the topic of "Process Governance". The responsible role for governance is the model owner (see 6.10: Roles in Model Development) named by John Jeston and Johan Nelis as the "Process Steward". John Jeston and Johan Nelis differentiate between different types of projects that determine the modeling effort, content, and means of expression used, as well as the modeling and governance methods to be used.

Project type	Explanation
Infrastructure	Improving the infrastructure to improve our business processes; Special focus on technical risk of the infrastructure project, special focus on interfaces
Package Implementation	Introduction of a standard solution as SAP; Special focus on costs; special focus on functionality of the standard solution and requirements of the company; special focus on maintenance and extensibility of the solution;
Bespoke system development	own development of a solution; Special focus on risks of requirement specification, planning and realization of the solution, special focus on costs
Legacy Projects ("Legacy system shut down, Legacy system consolidation")	Special focus on migration risks and unclear requirements

Table 18: Project types, see (John Jeston 2008)

Such classifications are helpful as thought patterns. Some time has passed since the publication of the book by Jeston and Nelis. I would, therefore, define the classification a little bit different today (wider).

Project Type	Explanations
Business Process Management Projects	Special focus on improving the business processes through non-technical solutions
Decision Management Projects	Projects focused on operative Decision Management; Projects about laws, regulations and optimization; projects with high risk on legal issues;

Table 19: Project Types (extended)

Part of the classification corresponds to the types of Jeston and Nelis. I made another distinction according to the type of development process. Classical projects, e.g. using UML and the Unified Process. We can build on a rich literature and big set of experiences (see, for example, (UML 2010) or (Kroll, Kruchten und Booch 2003)).

Building on modern platforms such as IBM® Blueworks, mapping business processes with BPMN or DMN to software implementations is easier and opens up new possibilities. The risk of lack of experience is reducing over time. Meanwhile, there are a variety of projects based on the modern platforms.

The class "infrastructure projects" I defined wider than Jeston and Nelis. This is not just about technical solutions. The introduction of RFID offered many innovations and opportunities for improving business processes. Not only technical innovations opens room for improvement, also organizational changes do.

I have added the category Business Process Management Projects. It will be highlighted in the next section.

6.9.2 Governance - Business Process Optimization and Business Process Improvement

In (Tregear, Reimagining Management 2018), Roger Tregear defines the two circles of Business Process Management: the Business Process Optimization (PO) cycle and the Business Process Improvement (PI) cycle. Figure 31: Process optimization and process improvement cycle (source: (Tregear, Reimagining Management 2018)) shows the idea. Business process optimization takes place as part of daily business process management. Process Improvement builds on this when we (fundamentally) want to improve the business process.

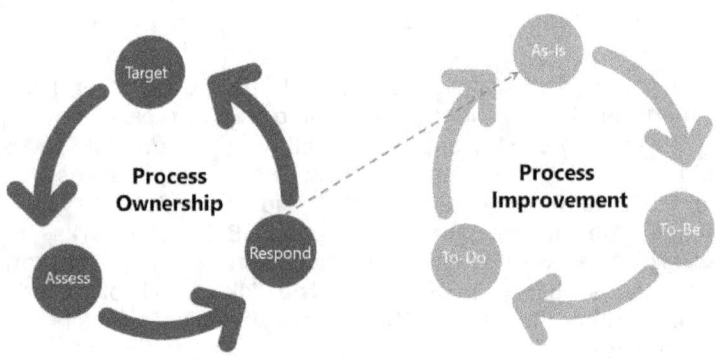

Figure 40: Process Ownership and Process Improvement Circle (Source: (Tregear, Reimagining Management 2018))

Business process optimization requires the definition of KPIs (Key Performance Indicators). Does our business process meet the specifications and expectations? In addition to the definition of the KPIs, we must determine the measurement of the values (value types, time, place of measurement).

Recently, the topic of "process mining" has become popular (see for example, www.fluxxicon.de, Signavio). However, checking the correctness and efficiency of the process is only one aspect of process optimization. If we do not use BPMN but CMMN and DMN, the process flow (the order of activities) is not the most important criterion. The focus of process mining is to verify that the (BPMN- or other flow-)models of the business process and reality are in sync.

To fundamentally improve a business process (Process Improvement), we build on the results of the process optimization cycle. First, we have to identify the possibilities of the improvements. Approaches such as Six Sigma ((Peter S. Pande 2014)), Lean (George 2003) and the resources for business process management in the bibliography are a good source.

Many of the tools support standardized or self-defined governance processes. For example, Qualiware, which for example includes processes for ISO 9001 and ISO 14001. Figure 41: Governance Process (self-defined, Visual Paradigm) shows an example of a self-defined process based on (Tregear, Reimagining Management 2018) in Visual Paradigm.

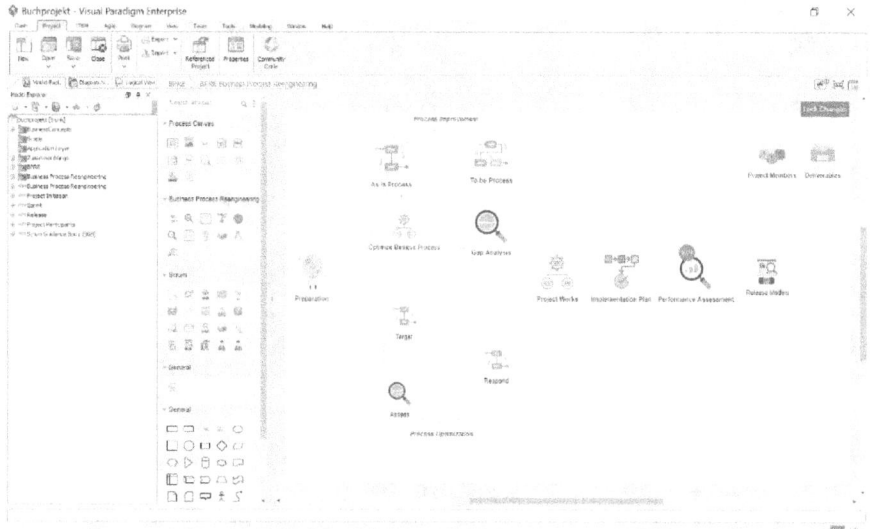

Figure 41: Governance Process (self-defined, Visual Paradigm)

6.10 Roles in Model Development

Related to the governance rules are roles in the modeling process. Literature and social networks often refer to the so-called "process owner". I do not like the term. However, it expresses the technical, content-related, organizational, financial responsibility for the design and implementation of the business process model. In addition to the process model, we use other models to fulfill our project mandate. That requires more roles. This can be a sub-division related to the content (for example, Model Owner Logistic, Model Owner Brewery, Model Owner Planning, ...). The sub-division can be related to the performed tasks (e.g. Risk Manager, Model Owner ISO-Certification, Model Owner GDPR). A task-related differentiation is thinkable too. According to the notations and concepts used, we differentiate, for example, process modeler, business decision modeler, system modeler. Agile methods do not favor specialization in the team. However, there are too many different tasks requiring different qualifications as a single person can combine all the necessary knowledge in itself. Each team member, however, should have an overall understanding. Scott Ambler speaks of "Generalizing Specialists" (Ambler and Lines, Disciplined Agile Delivery: A Practitioner's Guide to Agile Software Delivery in the Enterprise 2012). DAD differentiates between primary roles (always needed) and secondary roles (exist depending on the situation and may be temporary). Compare the definition of roles in DAD (Ambler, ROLES ON DAD TEAMS 2019).

Role	Explanation
Model Owner **Primary Role**	Responsible for models in our project Can delegate sub-responsibilities (e.g. Model Owner Logistic, Model Owner ISO-Certification)
Architecture Owner **Primary Role**	Defines the Business Architecture Defines Content and notations used Defines the relationships between the Architecture Elements
Business Process Analyst (Specialist) **Primary Role**	Describes the Business Process Models Decides on the notations used (BPMN, CMMN) Defines additional information (RACI, IGOE, other) Specifies the analysis method Defines Process Pattern to be used
Decision Analyst (Specialist) **Secondary Role (in case Decision Management is needed)**	Describes the Decision Models Decides on the standard notationen (DMN, TDM) and additional Descriptions (OMI, other) Defines Decision Pattern
Domain Expert/SME	Gives Information about Business Processes Checks Semantic Correctness of the Business Process Model
Model Tester / Validator **Primary Role**	Validates and ensures the quality of models
Team Member	
Stakeholder **Primary Role**	
Tool Specialist	Teaches knowledge about the used tool, helps to apply Style guide, Modelling Policies and the settings of the Architect Owners in the tool

Table 20: Roles in Modeling projects (source DAD)

Building a "center of excellence" is certainly also a worthwhile investment. The "Center of Excellence" has the task to examine new concepts and / or new tools for the suitability in the enterprise and to convey the necessary knowledge to the modelers. In addition, it accompanies project teams starting new projects in the use of the different concepts, use of the style guide and model policies, applying the governance rules, ensuring uniformity in the company. Above all, the "Center of Excellence" comprises employees of the primary roles, who can be "loaned" to the project teams as needed. The "Center of Excellence" does not have to be very big, requiring many resources in the company.

7 Tools

The book featured examples of several tools: Qualiware (www.qualiware.com), Visual Paradigm (www.visual-paradigm.eu), MagicDraw (www.magicdraw.com, www.dassault.fr), Signavio (www.signavio.com), DecisionsFirst (decisionsfirst.com). These applications are used by us in Projects and Workshops. For sure you find more interesting solutions in the Web used by us in Projects too. Examples are Adonis (boc-group.com), Intellior (www.intellior.ag), Semtalk (www.semtation.de), ARIS (softwareag.com) or BIC (www.gbtec.de). You find extensive documentation, e.g. (Visual Paradigm, Inc. 2019), (Qualiware 2019) und (NoMagic 2019) for the tools in the Web.

Users often ask which tool is the most suitable for me? The question cannot be answered without further ado. The answer is undoubtedly partially subjective. Several criteria play a role. Which one has the higher priority depends on your project task. The primary or only criterion is not, which notation is supported and is most suitable for my task? This is definitely a big advantage of the standard notations. The nature of the presentation and the meaning of the elements is standardized. In addition, the OMG standard notations include an exchange format. This allows the exchange between tools and platforms. No manufacturer can claim to own a better BPMN. The standard notation is supported or not. The implementation and support of new standard notations is often a temporary question. Other criteria are more important: ease of use of the solution, output formats and reports, the ability to easily add additional attributes not included in the standard notation (e.g. IGOE), proprietary representations, support for a role concept, and more.

- Price: Of course, the price question is always decisive. But consider that for very cheap solutions, the expectation of possible manufacturer support needs to be adjusted to the price.
  The tools I know support several licensing models: Single Seat, Concurrent License, Subscription Models.
- An important criterion from my point of view is the use and (full) access to a repository. A repository (inclusive full access) is needed to support the reuse of model elements, collaboration in the team (collaboration), as well as to structure the repository (and our project).
- The availability of a repository with full access to the repository requires knowledge and discipline. A full-access repository opens up many possibilities.
- Supported notations: Several groups can already be identified with the presented tools.
  - o Support for a single or a few standard notations
    DecisionFirst (DMN)
    Signavio (Focus on Business Process Management; Support for multiple standard notations: BPMN, DMN, CMMN)
  - o Universal solutions, suitable for many tasks and perspectives
    Visual Paradigm (support for many standard notations, UML, SysML, BPMN, CMMN, ERD, DFD, MindMap, ...)

- o Qualiware (support of many standard notations and means of representation: UML, SysML, BPMN, ERD, DMN, TDM, workflow models, ...)
- o MagicDraw (support of multiple standard notations: UML, SysML, BPMN, BMM, TOGAF, Zachmann, organization chart, ...).
- Supported platform
  Again we recognize different groups:
  - o Client-Server Solutions: Examples are Visual Paradigm, NoMagic, Qualiware. Visual Paradigm and Magic Draw can be used cross-platform (MS Windows, Linux, Mac). All known client-server solutions now additionally support the web platform. The functional scope of the web platform may differ (considerably).
  - o Pure web platforms: Solutions such as Signavio exclusively support the web platform. Especially when using the hosted solution, the cost of operating the solution is often low. The hoster takes care of updates and availability.
  - o Mixed solutions: Client-Server solutions with web-components
  - o Visio-based tools with repository: for example Semtalk
- Roles
  A tool must provide ways to support roles in the modeling process (see 6.6: Roles in the Modeling Process). The required notations and functions are limited depending on the role and simplify the use of the tool.
- Methodology and project management
  In addition to "pure" modeling, most tools support methods and work techniques. Examples are "textual analysis", "story boards" (visual paradigm), "risk management" (qualiware).
  All tools provide project management capabilities or support established project management methods.Examples are TOGAF® ADM (Visual Paradigm, MoMagic), PMBOK® (Visual Paradigm) and own project management methods (Visual Paradigm).
- Reports and evaluations
  It must be possible to evaluate the generated models and generate reports easily. Here are the web-based tools (yet?) not so strong. The fact that the stakeholders can all access the model on the Intranet / Internet does not relieve us of creating stakeholder-specific outputs and evaluations. Paper outputs are still relevant depending on the task.
- Quality control
  Beyond the simple syntax check of the notations used, it is advantageous to define and implement your own quality criteria.
- Code Generation
  If notations are used to describe system components (ERD, UML, wireframes, BPMN, CMMN, DMN), functions for code generation are essential. Integration with corresponding environments are frequently offered.

- Governance
  Ensuring timeliness and compliance plays an important role today. The tools, therefore, support governance functions.
  The supported features differ considerably.
- Multilingual Models
  Models have to be created and maintained in multiple languages.

First a distinction must be made between pure drawing tools such as Visio™ (products.office.com/visio) and Lucidchart (www.lucidchart.com). These tools are often easier to handle for the end user when creating visual descriptions. The combination of different views, as well as evaluation and analysis features are limited. Real modeling tools are evolving more and more towards architectural applications (business architecture, application architecture).

Table 21 gives a summary of the criteria for selecting a tool. Each user must determine the importance of the criterion for his project and his team and, if necessary, define further criteria.

Criteria	Explanation	Tool (Selection, Examples)
Platform	Client-Server	
	Windows	
	Cross-Plattform (Windows, Linux, Mac)	
	Web-Plattform	
	Mixed Platform (Client-Server with Web components)	
	Windows, Visio as Visualization-Component	
Supported Standard-Notations	Supported Standard notations (OMG, Open Group)	
	BPMN	
	UML	
	other OMG-Standard Notations (BMM, SysML, more)	
	Archimate	
informal Descriptions	Non-Standard Descriptions	
	IGOE	
	Mindmap	
	RACI	
Support for a Vocabulary	Support for a Vocabulary (SBVR)	
User Acceptance		
Roles	Support for roles in model development	

Method- and Process-Support	Techniques supported in the tool	
	Textual Analysis	
	TOGAF® ADM	
	PMBOK®	
	own Process	
	SCRUM, Storyboards	
Reports, Analysis	Creating Reports and Analysis	
	RACI-Charts	
	Stakeholderspecific reports in various formats(Word, PDF, HTML)	
Collaboration		
	Teamsupport	
	Version Control	
	Collaboration	
	Quality Control	
	Collection of Information	
	Governance	
	Release Mechanisms	
Task Management		
other Features		
	Generating Components (Code generation, DB-Generation, Generating Workflowcomponents)	
	Reverse-Engineering / Process Mining	
Mult-Language Support	Creating Models using multiple languages	
License Models		
Integration with other Third-Party-Tools	Integration with other applications as Confluence	

Table 21: Criteria for Tool Selection

All tools need knowledge. Workshops offered for standard notations and tools can be found on my web pages.

In case you have any questions or comments about the tools and the book, I look forward to your e-mail (book@model-based-business.engineering). I try to use the possibilities of the new technology (provision as e-book, frequent updates). Questions and suggestions help me to find out about your interest and to provide updates.

Part II: Blog-Posts and Short Essays

In this part of the book, you will find short essays and blog posts from my blog model-based-business.engineering on the topics of business architecture, notations, methods and working techniques, tools.

8 Visual Paradigm™ and Collaboration with Confluence ®

8.1 Visual Paradigm™

Visual Paradigm (Visual Paradigm, Inc. 2019) is one of the leading modeling tools. It features a variety of supported visualizations - from formal standard notations such as UML, BPMN, CMMN, SysML, SOAML, and others to informal forms such as process maps, mind maps, org charts, web diagrams, wireframes, and others.

In addition to the forms of presentation, Visual Paradigm supports many techniques and techniques (Scrum, Storyboards, TOGAF ™, PMBOK, others).

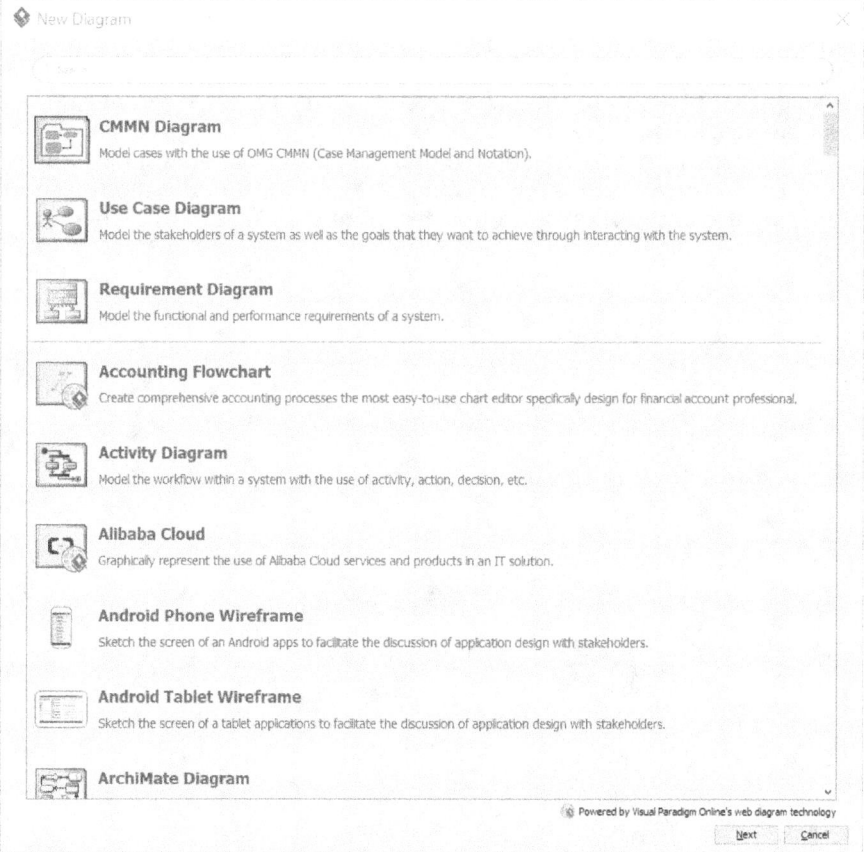

Figure 42: Presentationforms in Visual Paradigm

Components of Visual Paradigm provide Collaboration (PostMania component), Task Manager (Tasifier), and output to various formats (HTML, Word, PDF) (Component Publisher and DocComposer).

8.2 Confluence and Visual Paradigm

While users appreciate the power of Visual Paradigm to present content, they use other tools (such as Confluence, (Caldwell und Austin 2018)) to organize team collaboration for a variety of reasons (history, company policies, use in projects outside Visual Paradigm).

Then there's the question of how Visual Paradigm and Confluence can be shared.

In Confluence, "everything" (meeting notes, agendas, project plans, marketing plans, ... but possibly also models and artifacts from Visual Paradigm are stored in "spaces." Spaces consist of "pages." Pages can come in many formats: files, various files with various content, blog posts, links to the intranet / internet or a blank page.

So we can also integrate content from Visual Paradigm.

If we generate reports with DocComposer, they will integrate them into Confluence. If we use the publisher of Visual Paradigm, the output can also be integrated. In both cases, content from Visual Paradigm is incorporated into Confluence. The feedback possibilities of the team are limited.

The use of the PostMania component by Visual Paradigm is more elegant. In contrast to the integration of a link to the published page or a document created with DocComposer, here is a link to PostMania.

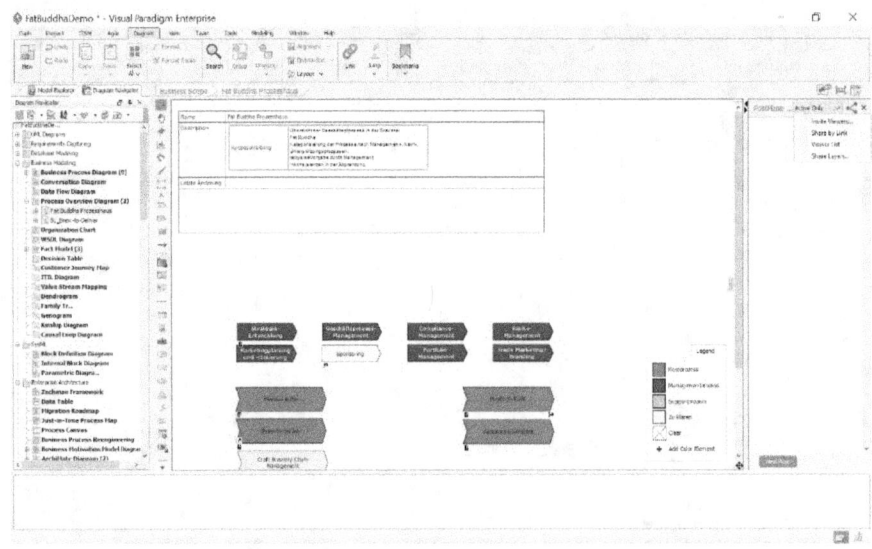

Figure 43: Creating a link to PostMania (Visual Paradigm)

By using the link, the user gives the possibility to view the models (in their current form), while PostMania offers the chance to comment on the model contents too.

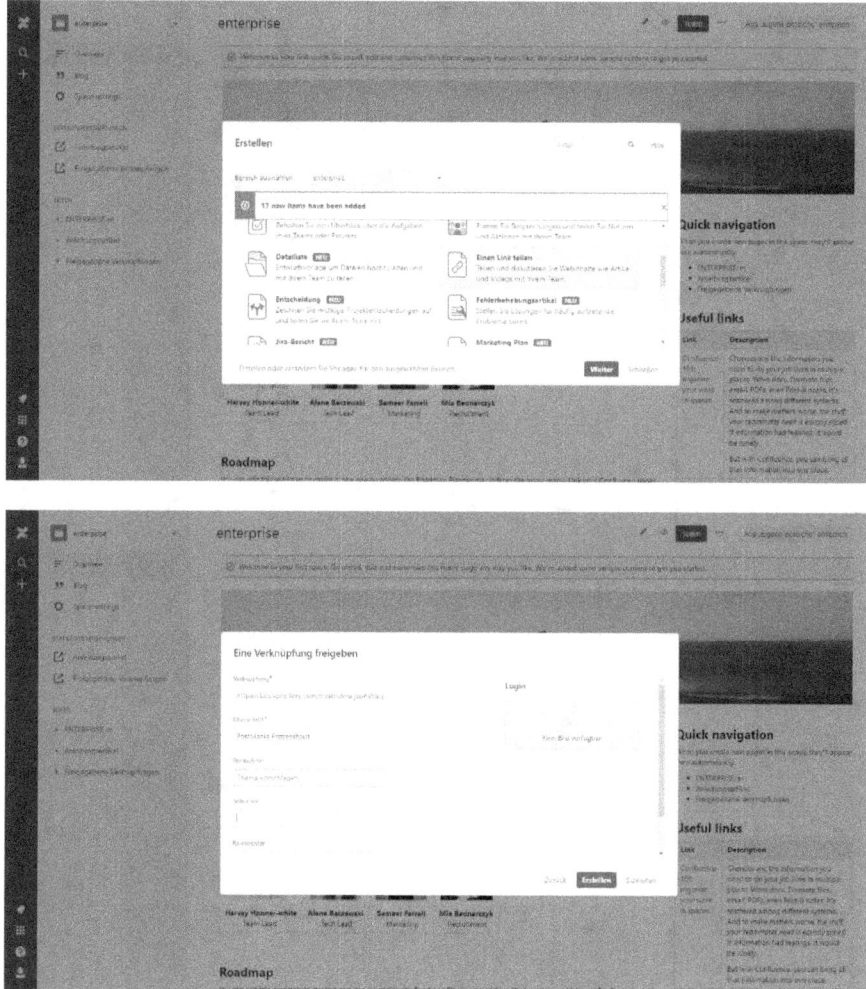

Figure 44: Release a link to PostMania in Confluence

113

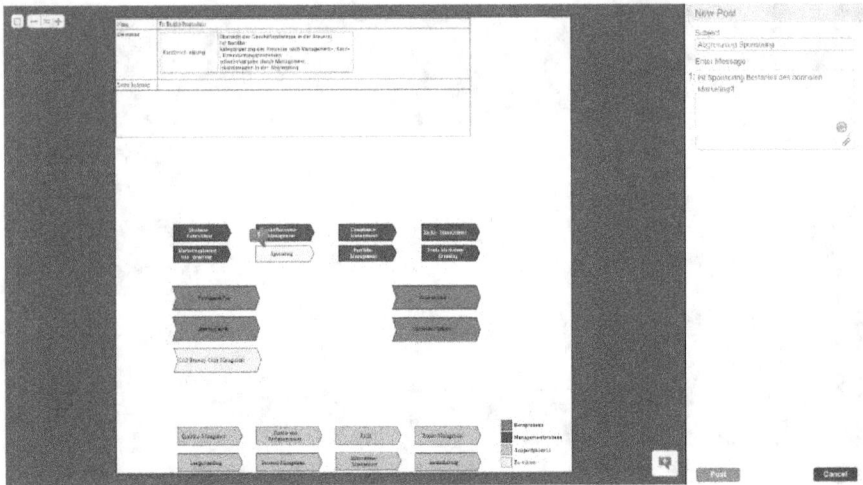

Figure 45: Adding a comment in PostMania

The modeler can "see" and edit these comments directly in Visual Paradigm.

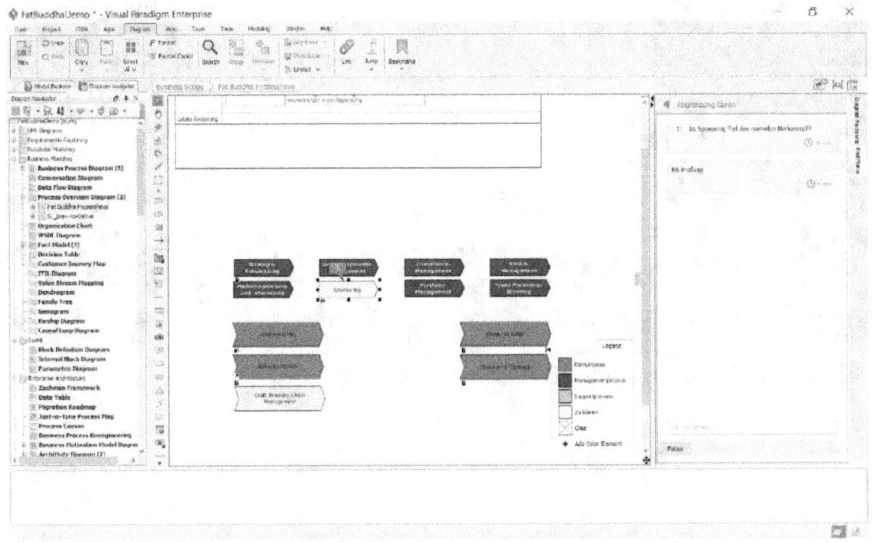

Figure 46: PostMania - Processing a comment in Visual Paradigm

In addition to PostMania, Visual Paradigm offers further options for querying links to elements and saving them in Confluence:
- Direct links to Visual Paradigm elements
- (HTML) links to published content

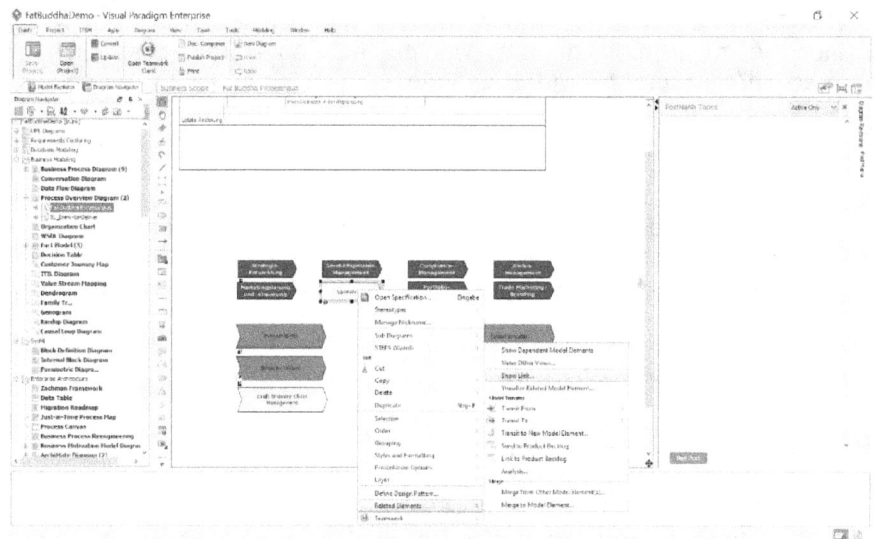

Figure 47: Querying a direct link to a Visual Paradigm element

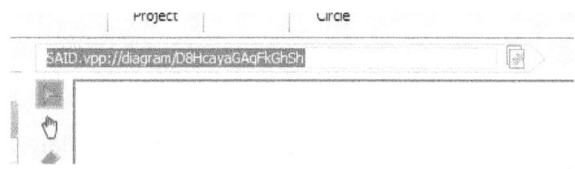

Figure 48: Using a Visual Paradigm link

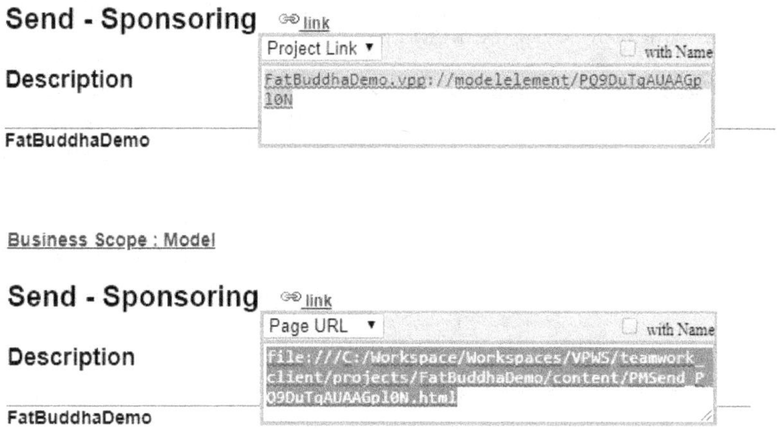

Figure 49: Visual Paradigm - Links to published content

As already stated, the variant using PostMania seems to me the best solution, because the elements can also be commented on by the user. Direct links require access to Visual Paradigm (If the links are used, the Visual Paradigm client should already be started) and the particular project. The interaction between the modelers is limited. When using the published content, we do not have the possibility of interaction/collaboration with the modeler.

No matter which method we choose, there are some questions to answer:
- How do we structure the spaces in Confluence?
- How do we structure the repository in Visual Paradigm?
- What content do we describe (textually) in Confluence, what content do we describe (textually or through formal models) in Visual Paradigm?

These questions are typically answered in a modeling style guide for the tools we use.

8.3 Manage the Media Break

Designing our modeling process, we need to make sure that one of the systems is up-to-date and the leading system for the different forms of representation (single source of truth). Otherwise, maintaining the media break is difficult and time-consuming.

8.4 Summary

Visual Paradigm addresses various tasks in the project (modeling, collaboration, project management). Although Visual Paradigm's various components (PostMania, Tasifier) cover similar tasks as Confluence, several customers prefer to use Confluence for these tasks. Reasons can be historical, may be in company policies or otherwise.

As explained in paragraph 4 (Manage the Media Break) the media break between the tools must be managed (style guide, modeling policy).

The statements made here apply in a similar way using other modeling or architectural tools (such as Qualiware, MagicDraw / Cameo).

9 Separation of Concerns and Levels of Detail

9.1 Introduction, Basic Architecture Principles

In my last blog post on enterprise-design.eu, I argued that complexity is a necessary feature of a (Business- or System-) Architecture to ensure stability, and "agility". Complex models require complex models and solutions. At the same time, no user wants to have complicated, unmanageable models.

Important fundamental principles to achieve the necessary complexity while at the same time avoiding complexity and ensuring maintainability is realized by the principle "separation of concerns" and the introduction of defined levels of detail. I look at that later.

Architecture Principle	Explanation
Separation of Concerns	Different content with different forms of presentation and different release cycles, belonging to different abstractions and level of detail, are shown separately. They relate to each other. Examples are business processes and business logic.
Defining Level of Detail	Levels of detail are used within an abstraction, e.g. to implement refinement or detailing. The levels of detail to be used must be specified.

Table 22: Important Architectural Principles (Selection)

9.2 Separation of Concerns and Architecture Frameworks

Several architecture frameworks exist in the market, helping us to organize our models and to implement the principle "Separation of Concerns".

The most important frameworks for me are the Zachman Framework™ for Enterprise Architecture (https://www.zachman.com/about-the-zachman-framework) and the Archimate framework (see e.g., https://en.wikipedia.org/wiki/ArchiMate). Both help us to decide which model elements are needed and how the elements are related. Both can be mapped to each other.

I am a "Zachman" fan because the framework is more diverse and, at the same time(in contrast to Archimate), it is method-neutral and can be used with all methods, of course, with Archimate or TOGAF too.

It separates "the world" in various abstractions: the "what", the "how", the "where", the "who," the "when" and the "why." A good model belongs to one abstraction. Different abstractions are connected, forming "complex models". This comprehensively describes the subject of interest without mixing the various views and rendering them difficult to maintain. E.g., business processes will be described in one abstraction (the "How"), used concepts of the business process are described in another abstraction (the "what").

9.3 Which abstractions do we choose?

Questions often asked in practice are:
- Which abstractions do we need?
- How do we present this content (Which notation or descriptive tool are we using?)
- How are the contents linked?

If we want to represent business processes, we for sure talk about the abstraction "how?". If we talk about the concepts used in the business processes, we talk about the abstraction "what?" But what about business rules and business decisions? One argument is that these artifacts are composite, the objects used in particular to connect different abstractions. On the other hand, the question addressed is the goal of the description. The primary purpose of a decision model is to give guidance. So I associate such a model with the abstraction "how?".

9.4 Several models in one abstraction

That is, in an abstraction we find several models that are related. An example are business process models and decision models. It is well known and admitted that we separate both aspects and not mix the description of the business processes with the specification of the decisions. Business Processes Models require the description of decisions too. Both are related.

9.5 Abstractions and Level of Detail

An additional question besides the assignment of models to abstractions is the question of defining detail levels. In my experience, too many levels of detail are often used. Contents are described unclear and too detailed. Models are difficult to maintain. When describing the original framework, John Zachman emphasized the need to define levels of detail. The specification of the framework makes no statements about the number and content of the detail levels. Merely the statement not to confuse or mix abstractions and levels of detail.

Users often ask for help in determining the level of detail. I think the magic number is THREE. This can be deduced from the number of elements (just consider how many elements arise depending on the number and complexity of the levels of abstraction). Different theories designate the levels of detail purely numerically, Level 1, Level 2. Level 3, etc. I don't think much of that. It is better to name the levels of detail according to purpose and target group. Then it is easier to decide whether we need the respective level of detail and the abstraction or not.

In addition to the number THREE, which results from the target groups, other systems are conceivable. If the abstraction "location" is essential for our project, the subdivision into the detail levels continent, country, administrative area, location is often used and sensible.

More interesting is such a structuring (definitions of levels of detail) that result from the content and the project order.

I use the following system for the basic levels of detail in "Business Concepts" and "System Logic" (see www.zachman.com):

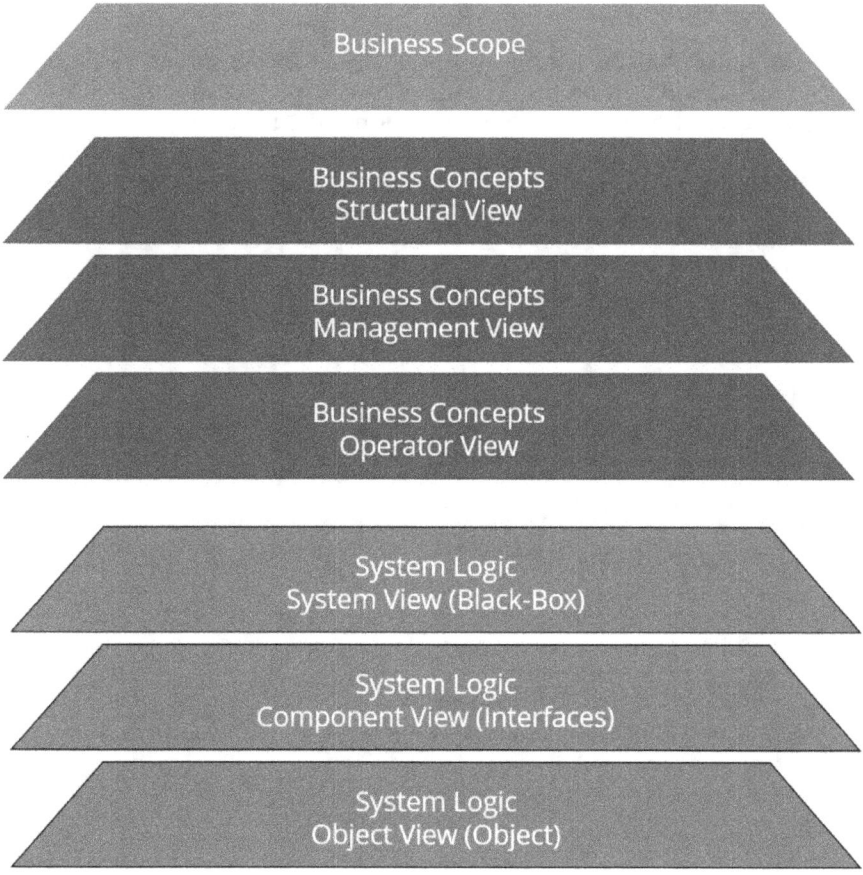

Figure 50:Levels of detail in the views Business Scope, Business Concepts and Systems Logic

Reminder: This is a Framework to be adopted, not a dogma. If we consider business process optimization in general, we may need all abstractions and levels of detail in "business concepts". Currently, many projects are underway to introduce the GDPR Directive. The focus is on the operator view (with the "Procedures of Operation") and the connection to "System View" in "System View" and maybe other views.

It is possible and typical to combine several principles. I prefer the principle shown above as the primary structuring principle. If necessary, it is supplemented by another (content dependent) principle. Example:
- Primary levels of detail for business process models: structural view, management view, operator view
- Secondary levels of detail (according to abstraction "location"): continent, country, administrative area, municipality

9.6 Tool Support

We need support for structuring in abstractions and levels of detail by the tools used. We need functions to refine models and model elements (we remain in the same type of model; for example, we refine a subprocess model again in a process description) or to link models and model elements (we change the model type to represent different views, different abstractions; e.g. we link a business process model with a decision model).

Good tools support these types of links. Qualiware or Visual Paradigm are examples.

10 Model Governance and Process Governance

10.1 Scope

Merriam-Webster defines "governance" as follows: "the act or process of governing or overseeing the control and direction of something (such as a country or an organization)". ((Merriam-Webster 2020))

In the literature, the term is found in combination with various terms or objects. We speak of IT governance, corporate governance (corporate governance), project governance, process governance, and also "model governance.

I would like to point out that governance includes the creation, maintenance, and use of the object of interest. Occasionally, discussions focus primarily on creation.

10.2 Create, Use, Maintain Model – Model Governance

I already outlined the general process of model development, use, and maintenance (see **Fehler! Verweisquelle konnte nicht gefunden werden.**).

Figure 51: General Model Development Process

10.2.1 Create Models

The collection of needed information and the formalization of this information is usually described and regulated in a modeling guideline and a modeling policy.

It describes which standard notations and informal descriptions we use, which working techniques are applied for information gathering and formalization, and how models are structured and built.

The question of model governance leads directly to the question of model quality. Figure 2 shows quality criteria for models (according to ((Rauh 1997) and (J. Pitschke, Model-Based-Business-Engineering: Successful Model Development and Use Notations, Methods, Techniques 2020)).

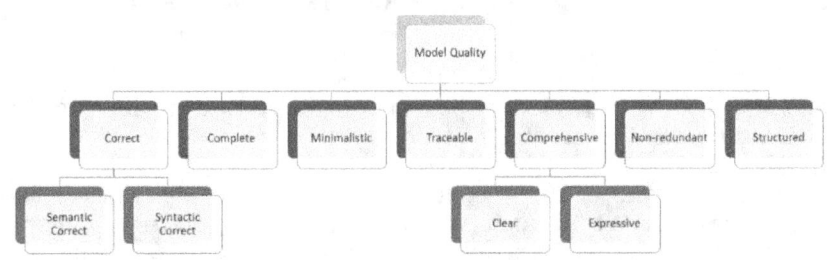

Figure 52: Criteria for Modell Quality (Selection)

Governance has the task of ensuring compliance with the quality criteria during creation and maintenance. Long-term maintenance, in particular, is often a challenge. The creator of the models is no longer accessible. The rules of the modeling guideline and the modeling policy have the task of ensuring and facilitating the long-term maintenance of the models.

10.2.2 Organizational Regulations

Organizational regulations are essential. E.g., the simple rule "After a year, the timeliness of the model must be confirmed by the model owner." We name a responsible role (the model owner) that is responsible for compliance with the governance rule.

10.3 Process Mining, Data Mining; Technical Solutions

In addition to organizational rules, technical regulations and automation is sought. The aim is for the models to correspond to the lived reality in the long term.

This is an argument for why repository-based tools are essential (see Chapter 7). These allow for reports and analyses.

Lately, Process Mining and Data Mining have become popular. Process mining is used not only for the long-term maintenance of the Business Process Models, but also as a working technique for information collection and formalization. The technique is powerful. The limits must not be overlooked. Other working techniques must be used in addition. In the literature section, you find suggestions for this. For example (Kaplan und Norton, The Balanced Scorecard: Translating Strategy into Action 1996), (Senge 2006) and the books on Six Sigma and other methods (((Peter S. Pande 2014)).

10.4 Design, Measure and Maintain Business Processes - Process Governance

A good model does not imply automatically a good business process. Maybe we have a perfect business process model that meets the quality criteria. However, the business process is ineffective, costly, and has other shortcomings.

In (Tregear, Reimagining Management 2018) Roger Tregear describes the PO and PI circle.

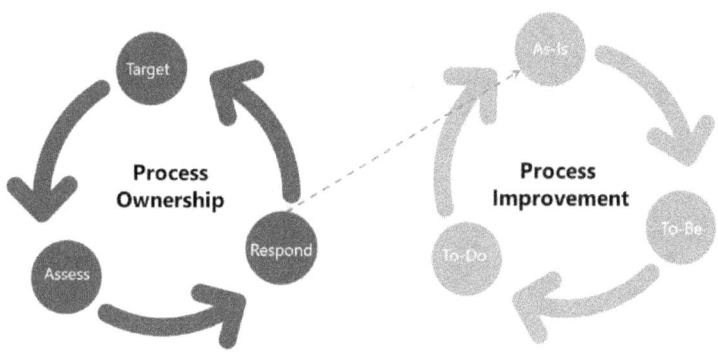

Figure 53: Process Ownership und Process Improvement (see Process Ownership und Process Improvement (see (Tregear, Reimagining Management 2018)))

Process ownership is an ongoing task. We try to manage the business processes continuously to keep them in-sync with KPIs.

Which role is responsible for this? It is the "Process Owner", not the "Model Owner".

The PI Circle is interesting from a governance perspective. What do we do to improve the business process when everything is fine, and there are no errors?

Linked to this is the question of KPIs. What can be influenced by the "operator" who lives the process every day?

If the operator cannot influence something, it is unfair to judge him and the process quality accordingly.

Here you can see the limits of Process Mining for the PI-Circle. Process Mining is based on actual data. We are looking for changes to improve business processes. This can not (yet) be found in the real data. Process mining often focuses too much (exclusively?) on the process flow. Improvements can also be found in the "enablers" used, business rules, and responsibilities (see 5.5).

10.5 KPI

Finding the "right" KPI is essential.

Once again, the "Zachman Framework for Enterprise Architecture®" I use (Zachman 2001) is helpful. What can I change and improve about a business process?

- What: I can change the business objects used. Both the business objects used as input for a business activity. But also business objects that serve as "enablers".

- How: The course of a business process (the flow) naturally influences the quality of the business process and is essential. This closes the circle to business process modeling. The operator often has little influence on the course of business processes. We model business processes to achieve uniformity, repeatability, assessability, ...

    The operator usually has a significant influence on the (operational) business decisions.

    Therefore, the modeling and description of business decisions (e.g., with DMN) is of great importance to the PI Circle (see (Taylor 2019) and (James Taylor 2016))
- Where: Sometimes, the "Where" has a direct impact on the process quality.
- Who: Representations such as RACI charts are part of business process modeling. Behind this is the knowledge that the "who" is important for process quality too.
- When: The "when" is also often very important. Processes in a nuclear power plant or an aircraft must pay due attention to the "when". Corresponding KPIs are part of the quality assessment.
- Why: Our project charter and our process charter determine KPIs.

10.6 Summary

Business Process Models are an essential enabler of Business Process Management. Therefore, governance of business process models and governance of business processes are closely linked, but they are not identical!

11 Language-Based BPM

11.1 What is the problem? The Model-Language-Gap

Business Process Management is an important topic today. Companies know that they need to manage their business processes actively. They need to describe, analyze, and optimize business processes. This is a permanent task. The environment changes permanently – we see new regulations, new technology, new opportunities coming up.

Processes are complex. We need to describe processes from different views and for various purposes to enable analysis and optimization. We use visual models for this based on standard notations as BPMN (Business Process Model and Notation, (BPMN 2.0 2010)) and DMN (Decision Model and Notation, (DMN 1.2 2019)). A single notation is not able to show all views and details we are interested in. We have to combine different notations. A good BPMN model should be based on a business vocabulary. The vocabulary holds the terms and facts used in naming and describing model elements in the process model. The SBVR (Semantics of Business Vocabulary and Rules, (SBVR 2008)) standard defines the elements of a vocabulary. The Business Process activities reference Business Rules described using SBVR or Decision Models using DMN. The activities in the business process are linked to business requirements describing the needs for the activity. Business activities are linked to requirements for the IT implementation.

Models serve multiple purposes (see 1.1: Model-Based ...)
1. Models are used for communication. We communicated the As-Is state of the process, the To-Be state; we communicate requirements, details, etc. for the business process.
2. We use models as a base for the implementation of IT systems. We generate system components from models.

Especially in the context of business analysis models are used for communication between different people – between subject matter experts, business analysts and stakeholders, business analysts and IT experts, management and operations.

In this context, we experience the "Model-Language-Gap":
- Language-based descriptions are the base for model development. We collect information and transform them into formal models.
- The models need to be translated back into language to analyze and review the models.

Often the transformation of the model back into language and the original information are not identical or even worse – they are really different. This is what I call the Model-Language-Gap. In the process of transforming language-based information into formal, visual models we lose information and meaning. This is a phenomenon know from Requirements Management, but it is also true for Business Process Management or Business Rule Management. The gap is especially a problem when the creator and the user of the model are different people or stakeholders.

The book contains different working techniques helping to transform unstructured, language-based information into formal models systematically (for example Textual Analysis; Table 14,Table 15,Table 16). The techniques reduce the Language-Model-Gap but do not ensure that the models are correct. Language-Based-BPM is a step to minimize this issue.

11.2 Language based techniques in the Modeling Process

Models are based on Natural Language.

The value of Textual Analysis and related working techniques is a systematic approach for the forward engineering of models. Different team members should come up with similar and repeatable models when confronted with the same information. Textual analysis narrows the model-language-gap. Textual Analysis is combined with other techniques as "Target Questions".

Textual Analysis doesn't answer the reverse question: How can we make sure that the formal model still reflects the original information? The model and the textual information are not necessarily in sync.

Natural language is used in many other places within business models. We describe the details of an activity, we use story boards to describe scenarios within a process, we use regulated natural language to describe business rules or business requirements. All such information should be created using the Business Vocabulary.

11.3 Language-Based-BPM – Synchronizing Language Presentation and Visual Models

Language-Based-BPM, in short, is the next step to minimize the Model-Language-Gap. We extend the named techniques to translate the created visual models back into natural language. The formal presentation of the model and the textual description of the model are hold in permanent sync this way. The modeler receives continuous feedback if the created model is semantically correct with regard to the original information by comparing the original information with the language-based representation of the model. This ensures the semantic correctness of the model. We have a permanent round-trip-engineering between the original information and the created model. We need tools supporting this to make the approach practical.

USoft Suite is the first tool in the category of Language-Based BPM. USoft focuses mainly on language intense models: Business Requirements, Business Rules, and Business Processes. USoft supports forward engineering – your natural language input is analyzed and transformed. USoft also supports the reverse step: The BPMN based process models are translated back into natural language.

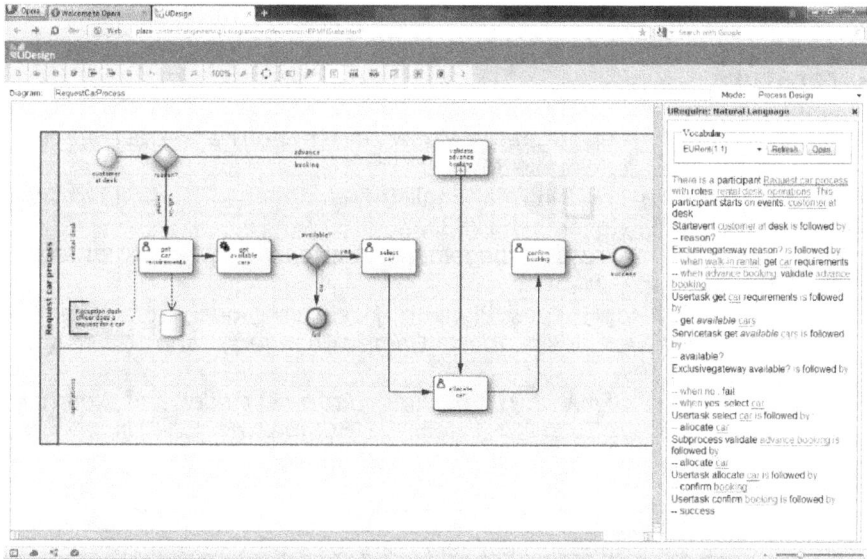

Figure 54: Visual BPMN-Model and Textual Description in USoft

For questions about the approach or USoft please contact me at info@enterprise-design.eu.

11.4 Low-Code – Backend-First

USoft extended the approach. USoft uses a "low-code, back-end-first" approach . From the business vocabulary and business rules, the low code, backend-first approach can be used to create complex applications with little IT knowledge. Of course, this also includes the font end.

Literature

Abbott, Russel J. *An Integrated Approach to Software Development.* John Wiley & Sons, 1986.

—. "Program Design by Informal English Descriptions." *Communications of the ACM*, November 1983.

ABPMP. *Business Process Management Common Body Of Knowledge.* CreateSpace, 2009.

Alexander Osterwalder, Yves Pigneur. *Business Model Generation: A Handbook for Visionaries, Game Changers, and Challenger.* Wiley, 2010.

Allweyer, Thomas. *BPMN 2.0 - Business Process Model and Notation: Einführung in den Standard für die Geschäftsprozessmodellierung.* 2. Auflage. Books on Demand, 2009.

Ambler, Scott W. *ROLES ON DAD TEAMS.* 2019. http://disciplinedagiledelivery.com/roles-on-dad-teams/.

—. *The Elements of UML 2.0 Style.* Cambridge University Press, 2005.

Ambler, Scott W., and Mark Lines. *Disciplined Agile Delivery: A Practitioner's Guide to Agile Software Delivery in the Enterprise.* IBM Press, 2012.

Barbara von Halle, Larry Goldberg. *The Decision Model: A Business Logic Framework Linking Business and Technology .* Taylor & Francis Ltd., 2009.

BCS - Juergen Pitschke. *www.enterprise-design.eu.* 2012. https://www.enterprise-design.eu/en/knowhow/enterprise-architecture-and-enterprise-models-resources (accessed 2019).

"BCS - Dr. Juergen Pitschke." 2006. https://www.enterprise-design.eu/files/images/downloads-wissen/bpmn_ba_a3.pdf.

Bens, Ingrid. *Facilitating with Ease!: Core Skills for Facilitators, Team Leaders and Members, Managers , Consultants, and Trainers.* John Wiley & Sons, 2005.

—. *Facilitation at a Glance!: Your Pocket Guide to Facilitation (Memory Jogger).* GOAL QPC, 2012.

BMM. *Business Motivation Model, Version 1.1, OMG Document Number: formal/2010-05-01.* Object Management Group, 2010.

Bono, Edward de. *Six Thinking Hats.* Back Bay Books, 1999.

Booch, Grady, James Rumbaugh, and Ivar Jacobson. *The Unified Modeling Language User Guide.* 2. Auflage. Amsterdam: Addison-Wesley Longman, 2005.

BPMN 2.0. *Business Process Model and Notation (BPMN), Version 2.0, OMG Document Number: dtc/2010-06-05.* Object Management Group, 2010.

Burlton, Roger. *Business Process Management: Profiting From Process.* Sams, 2001.

Business Architecture Guild. *A Guide to the Business Architecture Body of Knowledge™ (BIZBOK™ Guide).* 2013.

—. *Business Architecture Body of Knowledge® (BIZBOK® Guide) 7.5 (Appendix A Glossary - for A Guide to the Business Architecture*

Body of Knowledge® (BIZBOK® Guide) 7.5). July 2019. https://www.businessarchitectureguild.org/page/002.
Caldwell, Terrence, and Jamey: Confluence 101: Getting started in Confluence Austin. *Altlassian.* 2018. Caldwell, Terrence; Austin, Jamey: Confluenhttps://www.atlassian.com/dam/jcr:438a8cda-b614-4af8-a6c5-2a3fc949b4a6/confluence-101-getting-started-in-confluence.pdf (accessed 03 30, 2018).
CMMN 1.1. *Case Management Model and Notation (CMMN).* formal/2016-12-01. OMG, December 2016.
Debra Paul, Donald Yates (Eds.). *Business Analysis.* British Computer Society, 2006.
DeMarco, Tom. *Structural analysis and system specification.* New York: Prentice-Hall, 1979.
DMN 1.2. *Decision Model and NotationTM.* OMG, 2019.
Ebert, Christof. *Systematisches Requirements Engineering und Management.* 2. aktualisierte und erweiterte Auflage. dpunkt.verlag GmbH, 2008.
Foundation of IT Service Mgmt. Based on ITIL(R) V3. Zaltbommel: Van Haren Publishing, 2007.
George, Michael L. *Lean Six SIGMA for Service: How to Use Lean Speed and Six Sigma Quality to Improve Services and Transactions .* McGraw-Hill, 2003.
Hammer, Michael, and James Champy. *Reengineering the Corporation.* HarperBusiness, 1993.
Harmon, Paul. *Business Process Change, Second Edition: A Guide for Business Managers and BPM and Six Sigma Professionals.* Morgan Kaufmann, 2007.
Howard Smith, Peter Fingar. *Business Process Management: The Third Wave.* Meghan Kiffer Press, 2006.
IDEF0. *Integration Definition for Function Modeling (IDEF0).* Department of Commerce, National Institute of Standards and Technology, Computer Systems Laboratory, 1993.
James Taylor, Jan Purchase. *Real-world Decision Modeling with DMN.* MEGAN-KIFFER PR/EC CUBED, 2016.
John Jeston, Johan Nelis. *Management by Process: A Practical Road-map to Sustainable Business Process Management .* Routledge , 2008.
Kaplan, Robert S., and David Norton. *The Balanced Scorecard: Translating Strategy into Action.* Harvard Business Press, 1996.
Kaplan, Robert S., and David P. Norton. *Strategy Maps: Converting Intangible Assets into Tangible Outcomes.* Harvard Business Press, 2004.
Kemsley, Sandy. "Case Management and BPM (White Paper)." 2012.
Kroll, Per, Philippe Kruchten, and Grady Booch. *The Rational Unified Process Made Easy: A Practitioner's Guide to the RUP.* Addison-Wesley Professional, 2003.
Lines Mark, Ambler Scott W. *Introduction to Disciplined Agile Delivery.* CreateSpace Independent Publishing Platform, 2018.
Martin Sykes, A. Nicklas Malik. MarkD. West. *Stories that Move Mountains: Storytelling and Visual Design for Persuasive Presentations.* John Wiley & Sons, 2012.

Merriam-Webster. *Merriam-Webster.com Dictionary.* 2020. https://www.merriam-webster.com/dictionary/governance (accessed Juni 9, 2020).

Nohr, Holger, and Alexander W. Roos. "Informationstechnik und Prozessmanagement - Integration im Broadcast." In *Prozess und IT-Management in der Broadcast-Industrie*, by Holger Nohr and Alexander W. (Hrsg.) Roos, 13-34. Berlin: Logos Verlag, 2007.

NoMagic. *NoMagic-Dcumentation.* 08 13, 2019. https://docs.nomagic.com/display/NMDOC/No+Magic+Documentation (accessed 08 13, 2019).

Object Managment Group. *Value Delivery Modeling Language, Version 1.1.* 2018.

OMG. *Business Process Model and Notation (BPMN) Version 2.0.2.* OMG-Standardnotation, Object Management Group, OMG Document Number: formal/2013-12-09, 2016.

Ould, Martyn A. *Business Process Management: A Rigorous Approach.* British Computer Society, 2005.

Peter S. Pande, Robert P. Neuman, Roland Cavanaugh. *The Six Sigma Way: How to Maximize the Impact of Your Change and Improvement Efforts.* McGraw-Hill, 2014.

Pitschke, Dr. Juergen. *White Paper "Confluence und Visual Paradigm nutzen".* 2019. https://model-based-business.engineering/wissen-tools-events/mbbe-wissen (accessed Juli 21, 2019).

Pitschke, Dr. Jürgen. "BCS - Dr. Juergen Pitschke." 2012. https://www.enterprise-design.eu/wissen/business-process-management (accessed 05 21, 2019).

Pitschke, Juergen. *Model-Based Business Engineering: Successful Model Development and Use.* Amazon.com Services LLC, 2019.

—. *Model-Based-Business-Engineering: Successful Model Development and Use Notations, Methods, Techniques.* Independently published, 2020.

Pitschke, Jürgen. *Unternehmensmodellierung für die Praxis: Band 1: Eine Einführung in die Darstellung von Unternehmensmodellen.* Books on Demand, 2011.

Pitschke, Jürgen, and Ronald G. Ross. *RuleSpeak Satzformen, Business Rules in natürlich sprachlichem Deutsch spezifizieren, Version 1.2.* BCS - Dr. Jürgen Pitschke, 2009.

—. *RuleSpeak® Guidelines- Grundlagen, Version 1.2.* BCS - Dr. Jürgen Pitschke, 2009.

Project Management Institute. *A guide to the Project Management Body of Knowledge (PMBOK guide).* Project Management Institute, 5th Edition 2013.

Qualiware. *Qualiware - Center of Excellence.* 2019. https://coe.qualiware.com/ (accessed 08 13, 2019).

Rauh, Stickel. *Konzeptuelle Datenmodellierung.* Teubner Verlag, 1997.

Roger T. Burlton, Ronald G. Ross, John A. Zachman. "The Business Agility Manifesto." 2017. https://busagilitymanifesto.org/ (accessed Mai 15, 2019).

Ronald G. Ross, Gladys S.W. Lam. *Building Business Solutions - Business Analysis with Business Rules.* Business Rule Solutions Inc., 2015.

Ross, Ronald G. *Business Rule Concepts*. Third Edition. Business Rule Solutions, LLC, 2009.

Rummler, Geary A., and Alan P. Brache. *Improving Performance: How to Manage the White Space in the Organization Chart*. 2nd edition. Jossey-Bass, 1995.

Rupp, Chris. *Requirements-Engineering und -Management: Professionelle, iterative Anforderungsanalyse für die Praxis*. Hanser Fachbuch, 2009.

Rupp, Chris, Stefan Queins, and Barbara Zengler. *UML 2 glasklar. Praxiswissen für die UML-Modellierung*. 3. aktualisierte Auflage. Hanser Fachbuch, 2007.

SBVR. *Semantics of Business Vocabulary and Business Rules (SBVR), v1.0, OMG Document Number: formal/2008-01-02*. Object Management Group, 2008.

Senge, Peter. *The Fifth Discipline*. 1. Currency, 2006.

Serge Schiltz, Grace Dobler-Kim. *Holistic business process management*. processCentric GmbH, 2017.

Sharp, Alec, and Patrick McDermott. *Workflow Modeling: Tools for Process Improvement and Application Development, 2nd Edition*. Artech House Publishers, 2008.

SysML. *OMG Systems Modeling Language, Version 1.2, OMG Document Number: formal/2010-06-01*. Object Management Group, 2010.

Taylor, James. *Decision Mangement Manifesto*. 01 2014. http://www.decisionmanagementsolutions.com/what-is-decision-management/the-decision-management-manifesto/ (accessed 09 24, 2019).

The Open Group. *Open Business Architecture (O-BA) – Part I (Open Group Preliminary Standard*. 2016.

—. *TOGAF® Version 9.1*. Van Haren Publishing, 2011.

Tregear, Roger. "Business Rule Journal. Vol.20, No.5." *Roger Tregear, "Measure — Measure — Measure" Business Rules Journal Vol. 20, No. 5, (May 2019)*. Mai 2019. http://www.brcommunity.com/a2019/b992.html (accessed May 11, 2019).

—. *Reimagining Management*. BLURB INC., 2018.

UML. *OMG Unified Modeling LanguageTM (OMG UML), Superstructure Version 2.3, OMG Document Number: formal/2010-05-05*. Object Management Group, 2010.

Visual Paradigm, Inc. *Visual Paradigm User Guides*. 03 2019. https://www.visual-paradigm.com/support/documents (accessed 03 30, 2019).

Wilkinson, Nancy M. *Using CRC Cards: An Informal Approach to Object-Oriented Development (SIGS: Advances in Object Technology)*. Cambridge University Press, 1997.

Zachman, John A. *The Zachman Framework For Enterprise Architecture: Primer for Enterprise Engineering and Manufacturing*. Zachman Framework Associates, 2001.

12 Index

Adding Details 81
Agility 78
Architecture Principles 84, 86
BMM (Business Motivation Model) 32
BPMN 50
Burlton Hexagon 17, 18, 71
Business Capabilities 17
Business Decisions 58
Business Motivation Model 40
Business Process 50, 52
Business Process Centric Capability 18
Business Process Improvement 98
Business Process Model and Notation (BPMN) 32
Business Process Optimization 68, 98
Business Process Pattern 73
  Follow-Up 73
  Visual Paradigm 75
Business Processes 49
  Descriptions 49
Business Rules 58
Capability 89
Case Management Model and Notation (CMMN) 33
Classifications 82
CMMN 52
Control Activities 93
CRC-Cards 35
Customer Journey Map 68
Data Flow Diagram 35, 36
Decision Management Model (DMN) 33
Decision Table 60
Dendrogram 93
Detail Level 26
DMN 59
DMN-Element Decision 61
Doing Activities 93
Enabler 66
Enabling Activities 93
Entry Criteria 57
Exit Criteria 57
Governance 94
IGOE concept 65
Input und Subdecisions 62
Key Performance Indicator 98
Knowledge Model 62
Knowledge Source 62
Language Based BPM 124
level of detail 25
Logical Relations 82
Low-Code 125
  "Low-Code, Backend-First"-Approach 125
Methodology 78
Milestone
  Project Management 94
Model 13
Model Governance 84
Model Policy 84, 90
Model-Based Business Engineering 10
Model-Output 13
Monitoring Activities 93
Object Management Group 31
OMI concept 63
Operative Business Decisions 59
Organization Structures 70
Planning Activities 93
Primary and secondary Model content 14, 16
Primary Model Content 16
Process house 34, 38
Process map 34, 38
process participants 83
Project Charter 78
Project Management
  Milestone 94
RACI-Chart 66
Refinement 81
Relations in the Business Architecture 81
Risk 67
Risk Types 67
roles 83
Roles 99
RuleFamily Table 60
SBVR 44
Secondary Model Content 16
Semantics of Business Vocabulary and Rules 33
Semantics of Business Vocabulary and Rules (SBVR) 32
Storytelling 80

structure 23
Structure 21, 82
Style Guide 84, 87
  Example 87
System Modeling Language (SysML) 35
TDM 59
TDM methodology 64
Textual Analysis 90
  BPMN elements 92
  UML elements 92
The Decision Model (TDM) 33
The OPEN Group 31
The Opengroup AchiMate ® 3.0 35
Tool Selection 105
Unified Modeling Language (UML) 35
Value Delivery Model 39
Value Delivery Modeling Language 34
VDML 34
Vocabulary
  Community 44
  Fact 45
  Fact Type 45
  Synonym 44
  Term 44
Vocabulary 30, 44
  Concepts 44
Vocabulary
  Presentation 46
Vocabulary
  Term 47
Vocabulary
  Fact 47
Vocabulary 47
Zachman-Framework 23
  Content 24

13 Tables

Table 1: Model vs. Model Output different requirements 13
Table 2: Typical model content in the perspectives of the Zachman Framework (Examples) 16
Table 3: Simple Models and Artifacts in the Zachman Framework 25
Table 4: Types of Relationships in Fact Models 48
Table 5: Structure of Business Processes; BPMN versus CMMN 52
Table 6: Design Time versus Runtime 53
Table 7: CMMN Task Types 55
Table 8: Task Attributes 56
Table 9: CMMN - Eventtypes 56
Table 10: Risk Types 67
Table 11: Define needed Content 79
Table 12: Architecture Principles 86
Table 13: Structure of the repository (Example, Style guide) 87
Table 14: Textual Analysis (Abott) 91
Table 15: Textual Analysis (UML elements) 92
Table 16: Textual Analysis (BPMN elements) 92
Table 17: Activity Categories (Source: (Debra Paul 2006)) 93
Table 18: Project types, see (John Jeston 2008) 96
Table 19: Project Types (extended) 97
Table 20: Roles in Modeling projects (source DAD) 100
Table 21: Criteria for Tool Selection 105
Table 22: Important Architectural Principles (Selection) 115

14 Figures

Figure 1: Quality Criteria for Models 15
Figure 2: Primary and secondary Model content 16
Figure 3: Burlton Hexagon to describe a Business Process Centric
  Capability 18
Figure 4: The Zachman Framework™ 23
Figure 5: The Qualiware EA Framework 24
Figure 6: Using TOGAF ADM® in NoMagic 26
Figure 7: Level of Detail (BCS-Framework) 27
Figure 8: Structural Level of Business Process "Seafreight Import" 28
Figure 9: Management Level of process "Seafreight import" 28
Figure 10: Quality Criteria for Model Assessment 31
Figure 11: Notations for Enterprise Models 31
Figure 12: DMN Example (Qualiware) 34
Figure 13: TDM Example (Qualiware) 34
Figure 14: Example ArchiMate (Visual Paradigm) 36
Figure 15: Sample Process House Fat Buddha (Visual Paradigm) 38
Figure 16: Value Delivery Model (Source Visual Paradigm) 39
Figure 17: Overview of BMM 40
Figure 18: Motivation of FatBuddha described using BMM (Visual
  Paradigm) 41
Figure 19: Motivational Elements in Archimate® 42
Figure 20: Logical Progression through BMM 42
Figure 21: Fact Model (Example, Visual Paradigm) 46
Figure 22: BPMN-Palette (selected elements) 51
Figure 23: CMMN Palette 54
Figure 24: DMN Examples in Decisions First and Signavio 59
Figure 25: TDM Example (Qualiware) 59
Figure 26: RuleFamily Table in TDM (Qualiware), Decision Table in DMN
  (Signavio) 60
Figure 27: DMN Palette: Model Elements and Relations 61
Figure 28: Customer Journey Maps (Examples; Visual Paradigm,
  Qualiware) 69
Figure 29: Presenting Organizational Charts in Visual Paradigm and
  Qualiware 70
Figure 30: Competence-Capability-Resource Relations (Source (The
  Open Group 2016)) 72
Figure 31: Business Process Pattern - Follow-Up 73
Figure 32: Defining a business process template in Visual Paradigm 75
Figure 33: Describing a template 76
Figure 34: Brainstorming for CMMN-Pattern Return of an Article 77
Figure 35: Rory's Story Cubes (Samples) 81
Figure 36: Repository-Structure (Example, incomplete) 88
Figure 37: Use of References and Refinement 88
Figure 38: Use of a Complex Gateway (Example, Visual Paradigm) 89
Figure 39: Multi-dimensional Dendrogram (Visual Paradigm, Sample, in
  progress) 94
Figure 40: Process Ownership and Process Improvement Circle (Source:
  (Tregear, Reimagining Management 2018)) 98
Figure 41: Governance Process (self-defined, Visual Paradigm) 99

Figure 42: Presentationforms in Visual Paradigm 109
Figure 43: Creating a link to PostMania (Visual Paradigm) 110
Figure 44: Release a link to PostMania in Confluence 111
Figure 45: Adding a comment in PostMania 112
Figure 46: PostMania - Processing a comment in Visual Paradigm 112
Figure 47: Querying a direct link to a Visual Paradigm element 113
Figure 48: Using a Visual Paradigm link 113
Figure 49: Visual Paradigm - Links to published content 113
Figure 50: Levels of detail in the views Business Scope, Business Concepts and Systems Logic 117
Figure 51: General Model Development Process 119
Figure 52: Criteria for Modell Quality (Selection) 119
Figure 53: Process Ownership und Process Improvement (see Process Ownership und Process Improvement (see (Tregear, Reimagining Management 2018))) 121
Figure 54: Visual BPMN-Model and Textual Description in USoft 125

About the Author

Juergen Pitschke is founder of the owner-managed company BCS-Dr. Juergen Pitschke.

The topic "visual modeling and conception of enterprise solutions" has been his interest for a long time. Dr. Pitschke is known for his broad knowledge of the practical and systematic use of visual standard notations. His special focus is methodical approaches of enterprise modeling and their transfer into practice. He has translated the Business Process Manifesto, the Decision Management Manifesto, and the RuleSpeak® approach from English into German.

Information on training offers and white papers can be found at www.enterprise-design.eu and model-based-business.engineering. Feedback, questions, and comments are welcome at book@model-based-business.engineering.

www.ingramcontent.com/pod-product-compliance
Lightning Source LLC
Chambersburg PA
CBHW050008230526
45465CB00003BB/1308